DEVELOPING TOP MANAGERS

D0930752

WITHDRAWN
FROM B'ham-Sou.
College Lib.

Developing Top Managers

Alan Mumford

Gower

© Alan Mumford 1988

All rights reserved. No part of this publication may be reproduced, stored in a retrieval system, or transmitted in any form
or by any means, electronic, mechanical, photocopying,
recording, or otherwise without the prior permission of Gower
Publishing Company Limited.

Published by
Gower Publishing Company Limited,
Gower House,
Croft Road,
Aldershot,
Hants GU11 3HR,
England

Gower Publishing Company,
Old Post Road,
Brookfield,
Vermont 05036,
USA

British Library Cataloguing in Publication Data
Mumford, Alan
    Developing top managers.
    1. Executives — Training of
    I. Title
    658.4'07124   HF5549.5.T7

    ISBN 0-566-02719-4

Printed and bound in Great Britain at
The Camelot Press Ltd, Southampton

HD
38.2
.M85
1988

Contents

vi CONTENTS

PART III   THE WAY FORWARD

Preface

This book emerges from a combination of influences, the most important of which was the opportunity to interview a large number of main board directors about the processes which gave them the skills they use in their current jobs. Details of the survey and how it was carried out are included at the beginning of Chapter 1. The other main influence, which was also a check on the information derived from these interviews, was my own direct experience of helping managers to learn over the last 25 years.

The detailed interviews carried out by myself and my colleagues offered a superb opportunity to review how directors are developed. The development process, with its concentration on learning from real work, from the experience of managerial activity, will readily be recognized by directors and managers themselves. It will be less attractive to personnel specialists and management educationalists who operate from a quite different model. The consequences of comparing the reality of experience with the propositions of formal management development schemes are spelled out in the succeeding chapters.

The book starts with a review of the processes directors described as having influenced their learning. For most directors these were, in various forms, learning from real work on the job they had done. Formal processes intended to control or influence development were much less frequently encountered and often not so influential as the designers of these processes hoped. The reasons for this are analysed not only in relation to the particular learning experiences of directors, but in relation to the reality of management itself. By putting development into its managerial work context it is hoped to make it more effective, especially as the informal processes described by most directors have also been inefficient.

While detailed suggestions are made for improving the formal processes, the major novelty in the book is the identification of a new type of 'integrated but opportunistic' management development. This is a process which converts the informal and accidental experiences scattered through a manager's working career into experiences which combine successful task achievement and successful learning. The great virtue of this type of management development is that it enables managers to learn in the context they already understand, rather than one specifically designed for learning which they regard as less realistic.

The new model of management development presented here certainly requires a shift in both understanding and practice by those interested in structuring the development of managers rather than leaving them to learn in a wholly accidental fashion. It requires also a shift in the managers' understanding of the processes in which they are involved, so that they see the tasks they do as having a double content. The task remains the prime purpose of the managerial activity, but the managers are now asked to see that for some tasks for some of the time the learning possibilities can be defined, acted on and reviewed. This process is put forward with great confidence not because it is conceptually attractive (though it is) but because managers themselves recognize it as having been absent and believed (with no prompting) that it could have been undertaken by most of them. The attraction of the new model is not that it is novel but that it is deeply embedded in the reality of management.

I have written the book for three different groups. Since my research shows that current directors rarely read management books, it would be too paradoxical to aim it solely at them. Some will read the whole book; more of them will be prepared to sample the ideas and take personal action – Chapter 13 is provided for this purpose. Managers on their way to the top will be rather more strongly motivated to tackle the whole book, and will I believe benefit from checking their own experiences against those given here. Management developers, educators and trainers are challenged here to take a different view of management development and their responsibilities. The book shows them how to increase their contribution; but many of them will have to make a radical change in their approach.

Alan Mumford

Acknowledgements

The book makes use of material from a report for the Manpower Services Commission, published in 1987 as *Developing Directors: the Learning Process*. That material is Crown Copyright, and is reproduced with the permission of Her Majesty's Stationery Office.

My colleagues in that survey, Graham Robinson and Don Stradling, contributed substantially to the development of ideas which have found further expression here.

My colleagues at IMCB allowed me to spend some of my working time in writing the book, a luxury for which I am grateful.

Peter Honey gave me encouragement and criticism in an appropriate and helpful balance.

AM

Part I

How Top Managers Learn

The first seven chapters describe how directors have gathered their experience. The significance of the jobs they have done for both the 'what' and the 'how' of their learning and the contribution of structured formal attempts at development are discussed. The reasons for a lower than desirable impact are identified and proposals for improvement made.

1 Ways to the top

In this first chapter we look at the factors which seem to influence managers on their way to top positions. Subsequent chapters will describe the processes of development. Here the concern is with those personal factors which surround those development processes.

In Chapers 9 and 10 we shall consider larger scale influences such as the nature of the organization, its culture and the environment in which it is operating. The emphasis now is on learning and development.

Other research studies, and books without a research base, have attempted to review the characteristics apparently possessed by successful managers. Answers have been provided such as the need for power, the achievement motivation, the capacity to master change and the drive to search for new challenges. Whatever the utility of such explanations they are not the subject of this chapter or this book The issue discussed here is how people develop the capacity to direct the affairs of an organization, not what drives them to want to do so. The plan of the chapter is first to present the information derived from our survey, then to add to or comment on those results from information derived from other sources, particularly from other countries.

Participants in the survey

An author is faced with a variety of choices in presenting informa-

1

tion. My eventual choice has been to provide first the source of many of the comments made in this and subsequent chapters. An alternative would be to dismiss these details to an appendix. Either of these processes would suit different groups of reader, an immediate example of one of the themes in the book: individuals respond differently to the same learning process. In this case I decided to present the basic data first because I believe many readers will want to have that reassurance before being prepared to take seriously the subsequent comments. The whole survey has been published[1]; some details follow here.

We saw 144 directors in 41 organizations; 10 of the directors were women. We deliberately aimed at the highest positions in industry and commerce. The title 'director' is widely distributed at different levels in many organizations. In our survey, in all except a dozen individual cases, and for special reasons, the people we saw were at Main Board level, not directors of subsidiary companies or divisions. Some were from very large organizations like Unilever and BP but others were from medium and small companies.

We took total sales volume and average number of employees at the time of the last company report as our indicator of company size. We found that it was necessary to divide the companies into three groups in order to provide meaningful data. These groups were based on sales volume and are as follows:

	Sales Volume (millions)	Average Sales Volume (millions)	Average Employees
Group A	1–299	70	1 874
Group B	300–1 999	968	20 877
Group C	2 000–45 000	8 000	114 166
Total sample:		2 900	46 000

The companies within the sample were evenly distributed between the three groups as follows:

Group A: 14
Group B: 13
Group C: 14

We collected personal information about the directors we saw as follows:

Biographical data

The average age of the directors in the sample was 50. The youngest in the sample was aged 36 and the oldest was 63.

To give an impression of the age distribution in the sample we have grouped them as follows:

Under 40:	9.0%
40–49:	36.5%
50–59:	45.5%
over 60:	9.0%

The average age at which the directors had been appointed to the board of their present companies was 43. The youngest appointment to a board on which the director still served had been made at the age of 24 while the latest appointment had not been made until the individual concerned was 61.

Many directors served as non-executive members of the boards of companies other than that of which they were an executive director, and 16 indicated that their first executive directorship had been with a company other than that of which they were currently a director. The same may have been true of other directors but they did not specifically identify the fact to the study team. These 16 directors had taken up these earlier appointments at an average age of 34, nine years younger than the average age for the first board appointment for the sample as a whole. This might give support to the view expressed by a number of people in the sample that experience in several companies was a powerful learning experience which added to the director's credibility and effectiveness.

Only two directors were born outside the UK; one of these was non-white.

Of the directors in our sample 52 per cent were graduates and 50 per cent had a professional or equivalent qualification; 28 per cent had both a degree and a professional qualification; 16 per cent had neither a degree nor a professional qualification nor were members of any professional body.

The most strongly represented profession among the directors was that of accountancy. The areas of professional qualification represented were as follows:

Accountancy	30
Engineering	12
Personnel management	9
Computing	7
Management (eg FBIM)	6
Other (Legal, Pharmacy, Insurance etc.)	6

At the time of our discussion more than half the directors were currently holding a general management job either as Chairman or Chief Executive of a complete company or as manager of an operating division. In addition they had very often had experience of a wide range of functions; only 14 said that they had been limited to only one functional experience on their way to the top.

The range of influences considered

The influences with which we are concerned in this chapter can be grouped as follows:

Personal
    Early life and experiences
    Motivation and psychological rewards
    Financial rewards
    Current domestic circumstances

Environmental
    Climate for development in the organization
    Changes in the business

Planned or unplanned influences
    Scheme of management development
    Personal plans for development
    The right place at right time

Early life and experiences

We did not explicitly ask about experience which these directors may have had before becoming managers, but one of our early questions enabled them to volunteer comments if they identified such experience as significant. From our point of view responses under this heading were less significant since in most cases they were obviously not subject to choice in any sense that would be helpful to a younger manager planning his or her career. The information volunteered was however often important to the individual and of significance to our understanding of some aspects of their devlopment. Some of these pre-management experiences, recalled with such intensity 20 or 30 years later, remind us that the processes of forming an individual director are not only as widely varied as we shall see in this book but also spring from many levels of life experience.

We encountered directors from extremely varied family backgrounds. Some would be seen as highly privileged in the sense of relative affluence and acceptance of the desirability of, for example, university education. Other directors came from much harsher family circumstances lacking one or both parents, starting work at 15 rather than 21. For such directors explanations of how and why they developed started very early. 'My mother was widowed early and I was determined to do well not only for my own sake but much more for her.' 'My father was a clerk, but he knew there was a lot more to life than he had had and he was determined that I should know it and go for it.'

Some directors talked about early experience of responsibility when at school, but only one director actually identified the fact of having attended a public (ie private) school as one of the continuing factors in his development. Rather more directors said that university had been important to them, but there was a considerable difference in the significance of the nature of the degree. In some cases the degree was of direct practical relevance, for example in enabling a director who had read languages to undertake work first in France and then in Italy.

An even more profound experience for some of the older directors was their National Service. It offered responsibility and leadership which some believed had significance for their later career. Service experience of this kind is highly rated by some but rejected by others in considering the development of managers. It is unavailable on a large scale now, although small numbers of people with service experience still enter industry and commerce.

This first experience of leadership or management was sometimes recalled with surprising vividness. One director described how he first took charge of a group of soldiers during the conflict in North Korea. No officer was available within miles, and his sergeant was, as he put it delicately, incapable. 'Someone had to take charge and I did; that made me realize because I did it successfully that I could do it, and ever since then I felt able to take more responsibility and the next step forward and to think that I could grow with each job I took on.'

We asked all our directors at what age they had first been given management responsibility, and how important they felt it to be that this was relatively early or relatively late in their career. Most directors identified early experience as important; some thought it fundamental. Some of the people we saw had taken management responsibility relatively late, in their middle thirties rather than their middle or late twenties. They largely felt that they would have benefited from management experience earlier. This seems to suggest the validity of the view that early management experience is a good thing. We were however seeing those who had successfully survived early management experience; perhaps there were others who were broken by it.

Motivation

We acquired a lot of comments on the connected issues of motivation, psychological reward and ambition. Perhaps the most interesting was the generally expressed view that straightforward ambition to achieve Main Board position was not a primary factor. Not only did these directors not identify it but when asked questions specifically about it they stuck to their belief that it had not been a strong element for them.

A large majority identified a different kind of motivation. For most of them this was represented by a significant urge firstly to perform whatever job they were doing to a high standard, and secondly to take on greater responsibility. A rather crude view about ambition could be seen to be replaced by a more subtle and perhaps more relevant motivation – a desire to accomplish something, to do a job well.

Some of our directors could identify people with just as much ability, and at certain stages equivalent experience, who had not made it to the Main Board. This they attributed not to lack of ambition but to an unwillingness to surrender other values in pursuit of bigger and more responsible jobs.

The motive for development therefore was not ambition or title or status but rather a strong desire to take on more challenging tasks even when this meant giving up other attractive things such as domestic life, social activities and perhaps deep personal relationships. For many of our respondents the development that they engaged in was relevant to the things they wanted to do and not the levels to which they aspired. The rewards were not seen as directly related to success in learning and development, as specialists in management development might hope. They were seen much more pragmatically as rewards obtaining from the job itself, from the satisfaction of having learned how to do it well.

Financial rewards

The question of financial rewards is notoriously sensitive. Answers in this area are perhaps even more subject to question than in the other difficult areas already mentioned. Most directors not only ignored financial rewards as a possible contributor to their development but positively went out of their way to say so, though some recognized their significance during the early part of their career. It seems however that financial reward is perceived by most directors as wholly unimportant in their development at least in later years. (It may have influenced other aspects of their behaviour, such as expecting due reward for a tough job once achieved.)

Current domestic circumstances

In this predominantly male director population the spouse was usually a wife. A few directors mentioned the different kinds of help wives offered such as discussing career opportunities or accepting the need to move location. It was thought that there is now a reduced willingness either for husbands to request, or for wives to accept, a move for career interests.

Climate favourable for development

By climate is meant the extent to which the environment in which the director works encourages development. The climate for development requires a much broader range of questions and much more time than we could give it in our particular interviews. On the whole our directors had experienced a climate which they perceived as relatively helpful. There were very few comments about negative and unhelpful environments. One director however said 'It was more difficult to learn when senior managers were addressed as Mr and you were not supposed to raise difficult issues.'

References to a favourable climate related to organizations which apparently gave a very high and overt value to management development. A few organizations paid very visible attention to the process from the chief executive downwards, with a high level of personal commitment and a demonstration by personal action of belief in its value. There were rather more organizations where the climate for management development was relatively benign in the sense that it was accepted as broadly a good thing, that it contained some costs and risks, but without the sense of direction and purpose encountered in a few of the best organizations. In the vast majority, comments on these questions suggested that the climate was in effect neutral, giving no strong encouragement to (but equally no strong discouragement from) taking management development seriously.

Sometimes the climate changed dramatically. A crisis in a particular function or in the performance of the business as a whole could stimulate new demands and open the doors to new opportunities.

Changes in the business

Changes in the nature of the business, of the environment and of top manangement sometimes had a particular impact on the careers and occasionally on the specific development processes of a few of our directors. Diversification or acquisition brought changed demands for managerial skills. There were dramatic examples of businesses which had changed direction totally and in which managers not previously regarded as appropriate suddenly rose to the top. Sometimes the directors had been brought in from outside because too few of the existing staff were capable of meeting the new requirements. While it was clear that they had been recruited largely for their particular skills and experience rather than for the value of any development processes they had been through, it seems that some organizations are much better than others at facilitating careers, not only within their own boundaries but outside, because of the development processes they use. Some directors had of course acquired a range of experiences by moving around different organizations, not only between functions and products but in entirely different industries.

Formal scheme of management development

Chapter 7 offers a detailed review of the objectives and possible means of evaluating the success of management development schemes. This chapter concentrates on individual experience.

Many directors were not influenced by a formal scheme of management development for the good reason that none had existed when they were on the way to the top (or indeed in some cases did not exist at the present time). In other organizations there was a formal scheme. There were individuals who had been significantly influenced by the planned elements of such a scheme. Job moves were planned and implemented with careful mutual discussion; development needs were assessed and commitment to resolving them shared; courses with relevant content were attended at the right time.

However, the vast majority of directors we saw had not experienced a systematic plan for their development, either for acquiring particular types of experience and skill or for higher level planning towards an explicit career goal. If a scheme existed most of them thought that it had not been influential for reasons developed in subsequent chapters.

Personal plans for development

Formal schemes designed by organizations to influence development had not had much impact on most of the people we saw. In addition very few individuals had developed their own explicit plans for either personal development or career goals. Few had set out even in general terms to 'get to the top'.

A number of directors expressed some surprise that they had reached the levels they had. They may have been falsely modest: in most cases we could identify reasons for their career success. Most of them were there because they were either the most competent people to be promoted from within or the most competent who could be recruited from outside.

An alternative view is that these were extremely lucky people, with no particular claim to their jobs through ability. Particularly in the 1980s, and particularly for the kind of organizations we saw, this seems unlikely. We therefore took the view that directors had succeeded by a relevant demonstration of ability. Their surprise was justified and the element of modesty and humility understandable because there had been no master plan either by the organization or by the individual. We believed those directors who told us that they had had no career plan, though a few had possibly had plans which they were not prepared to admit.

Several directors commented on the difference between their own absence of a career plan, either organizational or personal, and the attitudes of younger managers in their businesses, whom they perceived as more likely to have explicit career ambitions. There was a greater requirement that the organization should be able to satisfy such ambitions in a relatively planned way. Their own development, on the other hand, was often attributed largely to being in the right place at the right time. Most of the directors however would claim the ability to take advantage of accidents. Sometimes they created a chance for themselves by visibility from successful performance. Some careers were advanced more quickly through unexpected retirements, resignations or even death; sometimes the people we were interviewing were the only possible successors for such jobs. For most of them development was a responsive and reactive experience, due to circumstance or to intervention by someone else, rather than a pro-active process initiated by the director.

The right place at the right time

Since formal schemes of management development seemed to have had relatively little influence it is not surprising that accident was quite frequently quoted as the reason for advancement. Changes in the business, especially growth, are accidental influences.

Although individuals may be unaware of the extent of organizational intervention in placing them in jobs, their perception of a relatively accidental process seemed very significant. They were

not accepting these 'accidents' as an ordained element in management, since many of them said that they were trying to ensure that
the careers and appointments of the subordinates were better
planned than their own. Perhaps organizations had been acting
benevolently but bosses and personnel directors had not in the past
felt it appropriate to tell people what was happening? This was not
now believed to be defensible by these directors.

Several directors said it was important not to be in the wrong
place at the wrong time. Some of their peers with apparently equal
experience and ability fell short of the board because their job had
very low visibility and excellent performance was simply not noted.
It might alternatively have very high visibility because of major
problems associated with it, and it was possible for a manager to be
blamed for poor performance which was outside his control. Others
got the credit for excellent performances similarly influenced by
outside factors. A particular activity or product or senior boss
might also be in favour at some particular time in the organization.
Just as some directors had secured quick promotion through the
failure of the boss, others might have suffered through being
associated with the failure of a boss or of a product.

Possible negative influences

We thought it possible that some individuals might have been held
back by unsuccessful experiences or a negative development
climate. Most directors were puzzled by this concept and there
were very few specific responses to it. Nearly all of them said that
any experience which might have fallen into this category, such as
working on a failed product, had more positive than negative consequences. Although such an experience might have been uncomfortable it also contained substantial learning potential. 'I was working
in a department where no one was allowed to make any decisions
without reference up at least two levels of management. It was a
very frustrating experience. I got away from it as quickly as I could.
For a time it held back my development I suppose but on the other
hand it taught me better than perhaps working in a more positive
environment might have done some of the facts of life about decision making, accountability and the inability of some managers
to delegate.'

Women directors

Only 10 of the participants in the survey were women. The Institute of Directors in October 1986 said that there were only eight women directors on the boards of Britain's top 100 companies. Being a woman obviously influences one's prospects of reaching the top job! The question here is whether the fact of being a woman influenced the development processes of the women we saw. In view of the comments frequently made about the problems women encounter in managerial jobs, it is interesting that only one made specific reference to attitudes to women as having been a negative influence. She said she still encountered resistance to her simply because she was a woman. Perhaps because they were high achievers the women generally gave little emphasis to any positive or negative factors based on their sex.

Some of the problems experienced by women in a male managerial world were, however, reflected in their comments. They may have had to struggle harder for their opportunities.

Views on influences from other sources

The survey was unique in its concentration on directors, and it is useful to check its findings against other research. The first linking point to the information we collected is the previous section dealing with women. Most of the literature about the development of women as managers describes sexist processes which inhibit their promotion. These factors are by now generally known although of course the consequences are not always accepted. Women are held back by at least two negative forms of behaviour by men who dominate managerial life. On the one hand it is frequently assumed by men that women are either not interested in a long-term managerial career or will allow marriage to frustrate any early ambition. On the other, women are believed by men to behave not only differently but less effectively as managers, and by not matching the male stereotype of effectiveness are disbarred from promotion and development. Marshall[2] gives clear expression to many of the factors holding back women. Research on the domestic circumstances of women and men is also very revealing.[3] In the UK 39 per cent of women managers were unmarried, divorced or widowed, as against 8 per cent of men. In the US the comparable figures were 42 per cent and 5 per cent. The comment of a woman manager that what she really needed was a home with a wife prepared to look after her is now quite well known. Presumably some women are not prepared to pay the price indicated in these figures. While the female contributors in our survey did not identify positive or negative influences related to their sex, it seems clear that the fact of being a woman has some negative influences on the number of women reaching the top.

Charles Margerison has produced two studies of influences on development as seen by chief executives.[4,5] He presented chief executives with a different list of questions from those used in our survey, but covered some of the issues dealt with in later chapters. Although the rank order was slightly different as between the UK and the USA, chief executives responded with high scores on the following influences:

> need to achieve results
> ability to work with a wide variety of people
> early overall responsibilities for important tasks
> wide experience in many functions prior to age 35
> willingness to take risks

These are the important shared influences at the top of much longer lists. There is quite a lot in common (although the questions are slightly different) with some of our findings mentioned above.

A study[6] carried out by the consultants PA in 1985 of the chief executives of 256 leading British companies identified four key periods for their development:

> first management job (identified by one-third)
> National Service
> first overseas posting
> business crisis or turnaround

Two of these bear directly on what we found. Comparisons are frequently made between the number of MBAs (Masters of Business Administration) produced annually in the UK and the USA (about 1500 as against 60 000). We found five MBAs in our sample, which seems in tune with information from other sources about the number of MBAs in British commerce at top level. A study published in the United States in 1980[7] showed that 25 per cent of all newly appointed top executives in this survey of 11 000 managers had an MBA. Whatever the arguments about the impact of MBA programmes, the fact that so many managers had attended such programmes in the USA would presumably register as an influence. However, the Margerison and Kakabadse study already quoted[5] showed job management training as twentieth on a list of 21 possible influences.

Comparisons nowadays are often made with Japan. A survey of 1000 Japanese companies showed that 40 per cent of their directors had a technical background. In our survey the roughly comparable figure of those with an engineering or computing qualification is about 14 per cent, so that even allowing for people with technical experience but no professional qualification a significant difference emerges.

Summary

Broad influences of the kind addressed in this chapter clearly vary considerably between individuals. Perhaps the most powerful impression gained from this survey, and from comparisons of the results with my other experiences, is of the influence of an individual's self concept. The combination of personal belief and habits and occupational views expresses itself in a sharper focus on one kind of activity rather than another. One expression of that was seen in a number of our interviews. A wish to do well, and then a wish to do even better, seemed to have pushed a number of our directors along the path to the top. It is interesting to reflect on the comments made to us about the importance of being 'in the right place at the right time'. Although a number of our directors referred to the significance of that, a number of them also said that you still needed to have the ability to take advantage of an accidental opportunity. This was rather well expressed in a review by Alex Comfort of an autobiography by Sir Peter Medawar: 'Fortunate accidents happen to the mentally prepared. We all have random opportunities – Nobel prize winners recognize them and pin them down.'

References

1   Mumford, A. et al., *Developing Directors: Learning Processes*, Manpower Services Commission, Sheffield, 1987
2   Marshall, Judi, 'Women Managers' in A. Mumford (ed.), *Handbook of Management Development*, 2nd edn., Gower, Aldershot 1986
3   Alban Metcalfe, B., *Career Development of British Managers*, British Institute of Management 1984
4   Margerison, C., 'How Chief Executives Succeed', *Journal of European Industrial Training*, 1980, vol. 4, no. 5
5   Margerison, C. and Kakabadse, A., 'How American Chief Executives Succeed', AMA Survey Report, New York, 1984
6   PA Consultants, *Corporate Leadership in Britain*, London, 1985
7   Swinyard, A.W. and Bond, F.A., 'Who Gets Promoted', *Harvard Business Review*, September/October, 1980, pp. 6–18

2 Learning from the job

'Learning from experience' is the cliché most frequently used by managers themselves to describe the way in which they have learned, and they mostly mean learning from the jobs they have done.

This chapter will describe the kind of experiences from which our interviewees had learned, and will comment also on some types of experience not revealed in the survey. I shall consider how managers learned from the job itself, as distinct from how they learned from other people such as bosses or colleagues while doing a job, which is the subject of the next chapter.

Learning from doing the job was the most frequent, pervasive and intimate experience of learning. The reason for this was well expressed by a famous American bank robber Willie Sutton. When asked why he robbed banks he replied 'That's where the money is'. Managers' perception of why they learn from doing the job offers the same kind of perception, 'that's where real learning occurs'.

Learning from job experiences was for most of our respondents an unplanned, relatively disorganized and unreflective process. Directors were able to perceive job experiences as learning experiences in discussion with us, often many years after the event. However, they frequently commented to us that they had not seen those job experiences as learning experiences at the time, a point on which comments are offered at the end of the chapter. The following analysis with its structure and implied boundaries between different kinds of job experience is much neater than the reality experienced by managers, and recalled to us!

The following are the opportunities for or occasions of learning changes:

The job as it is

Current content – relatively familiar
Changing demands within the job – caused by eg new objec   tives or techniques
Pushing at the boundaries

Additions to the job

Projects
Task forces
Special assignments
Committees
Junior boards

New jobs

Line promotion
Job rotation
Secondment
'Assistant to'

The job as it is

Current content

Since directors thought they had learned most from actually doing managerial work, the actual content of the jobs they had done was the prime influence on what they learned. Chapter 8 discusses the likely content of directors' jobs and identifies some of the differences between jobs at the top and those in the middle management. This chapter shows how the differences influence what has been learned. This seems to occur in two slightly different ways. Once the manager is established in the job, the main causes of learning may be either changes in the job content or demands, or changes in the manager's own perception of the job and the opportunities within it.

Even without changes in content managers learn new things because they attempt new things. Some do this because they need to improve even on good performance and want to be seen as high achievers. For example a manager may change the targets set for negotiation with a supplier, or decide to set up a new kind of management meeting, or instal a different communication process. Examples of this kind were most readily recalled by directors precisely because they were conscious changes with a cause and effect. The cause and effect were originally about management performance but could subsequently be seen as having brought about some learning.

One example concerned the process of introducing change. 'I learned that arriving on Monday with a fully fledged plan for what we were going to do was not a good idea. My subordinates did not want "my" plan, they wanted "our" plan.'

In this case the director thought it was a new situation, rather than a fault in his basic style, that had brought about learning. Other directors referred explicitly to mistakes and how they had learned from them. 'I used to want to win every argument that ever came up in a management meeting. I was much better in debate than most other managers present so I used to win most discussions. I learned that was a mistake when I found that the people I beat in argument then tried to make sure outside the meeting that I lost in other ways.' Directors quoted small-scale and large-scale experiences of learning from failure, ranging from an inability to deal with a persistent latecomer in a department to a substantial loss of money on a failed project.

The fact that managers learn from failure is not surprising; nor is it astonishing to find again that managers are prepared to assess the causes of failure and to learn from such an assessment. They are much less interested in finding the causes of success, as a balanced learning process would seek to do. Managerial priorities do not accord with this balanced view; putting things right is a managerial priority, whereas understanding the reasons for success contains few prospects of immediate reward.

Significant changes in priorities, the impact of unusual events, were the main causes of learning for most directors. A few learned from the more normal processes of management:

Reviewing Achievements and What I Have Learned
I tend to have two agendas at the start of each working day. One is written down and consists of a list of meetings, and probably tasks that I need to achieve during the day. The other list I sometimes write down but more often keep in my mind. This is a list of things I want to achieve during the meeting or through the achievement of the task. It is usually too time-consuming to write these down, but I have them in mind. At the end of most days I review how well I have done. I look as objectively as I can at what I have achieved and what my contribution has been, as well as that of others, to success or failure on things I set out to achieve. Again I do not do this very formally. I often do it in the train going home, or in the car if someone else is driving me. I sometimes do it over a drink in the evening or when I am gardening or riding at the weekend.

This director was unusual in his approach. He did not keep a learning log of the kind discussed later in the book, although exhibiting many of the benefits. The fact that he was unusual yet used an eventually uncomplicated process to good effect shows that the opportunities for learning within the job are not yet fully explored by most managers, yet are achievable by many of them.

Changing demands within the job

Job content may change because of changes in organization structure, objectives, priorities, development of new services or products, or the demands of a new boss (see Chapters 8 and 9).

A change in an organization's attitude to quality had brought about a change in the production manager's job in one case. He had previously been responsible for preventing defective products from leaving the plant, and his relationship with the design department was that he complained about their design causing him problems. He was now required to work with them on eliminating the causes of defects. 'I learned a lot about the design process, and also a lot about how you have to tackle adversarial relationships instead of letting them fester.'

Pushing at the boundaries

Although directors mostly disclaimed explicit ambition as a cause of development they were influenced by a substantial wish to 'do the job well'. Ambition may indeed have been an underlying factor of which they may not have been wholly conscious, since few of them can have been unaware of the fact that 'doing well' is frequently a cause of promotion.

The wish to do well expressed itself not only by improvement within current job content but by a process described to us by one of the directors as 'pushing at the boundaries'. He and others who described similar experiences meant something quite different from empire building. They were not concerned to take over completely another department's responsibilities, or to take over a project or an effective performer from another department.

In terms of personal development the process had probably rather different motivations and certainly was expressed differently. In these cases what was being described was a process by which a manager sought to get involved more in activities next to his existing job. This for example meant asking to attend certain management meetings, or volunteering to take up a particular problem. This latter was particularly interesting since sometimes the problem was a long-standing one or, if recent, was recognized as a hot potato. 'No one in my job had ever suggested before that we ought to visit the client. I did it at the time because I thought it would help us to tackle some problems. Looking back on it I realize how significant it was because I learned so much about what the client's interests were at first hand.'

Additions to the job

So far we have reviewed the job itself, and learning opportunities which arise within the job as currently accepted. This section concerns managerial activities added to the job as it is normally perceived.

Projects

Projects can arise either within current job content or as additions to it.

A few years ago I was given responsibility for investigating whether to set up a new company in France. The company would sell the same products that I was currently producing to the same sort of customer, and the probability was that it would report to me. The managing director gave me a briefing about why it needed to be looked into, and said he wanted a report ready for a main board meeting in three months' time. I learned a lot from the project. Certainly dealing with the French was a valuable experience which has come in useful subsequently. Even more I learned something about how to set up a project. I was given no proper terms of reference, no budget, and people I went to for help at senior level did not know that I was doing the project.

Other managers quoted examples sometimes better organized:

responsibility for investigating a new plant location
setting up a new production line within an existing plant
taking a new product from research into development
defining a new management information system

One of the distinguishing features of this kind of project is that the recognition of learning is stronger because of the novelty of the circumstances in which the manager is involved. Sometimes there is a substantial shock in terms of the new problems encountered and new relationships required with different kinds of people.

Task forces

While projects may sometimes be a group activity, a task force always is. It may include representatives from a number of different departments, so the range of learning involved for the manager may be extended not only by the actual content of the issue being addressed but by exposure to the priorities, prejudices and intelligence of other functions. It may be the first time the manager has encountered either the problems within the task or the interests of the other parties involved. When the task force gets on to implementation there can be a great deal of learning about how this is best tackled. One example was that of a manager who worked on a task force given the responsibility of bringing out two new products from three manufacturing plants which were at the same time making the existing basic profit earner of the business.

Special assignments

While projects and task forces may take up quite a lot of the manager's time, demands may stretch even further to the extent that a special task, rather than the normal routine of the current job, becomes the prime concern of the manager. We encountered a technical director who, while still carrying his normal responsibilities for current technical processes, was given responsibility for carrying through a pilot programme involving a technology totally different from the traditional form.

In projects or on task forces managers normally scraped through without any formal change in managerial responsibilities under them, whatever the additional time demands. In this case so substantial was the time involved in the assignment that new arrangements had to be made.

> We knew I would have to delegate more although to be honest I did not realize exactly how much of my time was going to be spent on the new assignment. As well as all the things I learned from problems of introducing the new technology I learned a lot about how difficult it was not just for me but for the people under me to have a kind of temporary reporting relationship. People did not really know who to come to for advice or decision. My subordinates and I thought we had agreed it quite carefully, but we had not really understood the problems that people outside would have. When I set up an assignment of that kind when I got on the Board I made sure it was explained more clearly.

Assignments, like projects and task forces, were most frequently set up with pure (if not clear) task objectives: the organization wanted a problem or issue to be resolved. Mostly they were initially undertaken by the manager on that understanding as well, in the sense that he understood his involvement to be about the successful completion of the task. Managerial issues arising from the task were less frequently understood and defined. For example the problem of introducing change, or influencing people without having direct authority over them, was either not recognized or not discussed in advance. Directors commonly said therefore that it was only with hindsight that they saw that such issues has arisen, and that they had learned from them. The implications of this for the effectiveness of the learning process involved are substantial. If the managerial activities themselves are not fully comprehended in advance, the learning opportunities which may arise from them will be even less likely to be understood and planned. Later in the chapter a process for at least partially remedying this problem is described.

Committees

For the purpose of this chapter committees are defined as groups of managers meeting regularly to discuss a range of relatively routine issues. This distinguishes them from the special groups set up for projects, task forces or special assignments. They were never identified as significant learning activities when they merely involved operating within the current content of the job. Learning was more frequently foreseen when a manager was appointed to a committee where the association with the current job was less direct. His presence on the committee might be due to the need to have a representative from a particular department, be a recognition of his potential personal contribution, or indeed occasionally be the result of a development plan. We encountered directors who had learned about financial decision making from being appointed to pensions committees, investment committees or new acquisitions committees.

Junior boards

None of the directors we saw had been involved in a management committee deliberately set up to mirror and give experience in the kind of issues dealt with at main board level. Some organizations use such a process as a deliberate development device to expose up-and-coming managers to a number of the issues and priorities for which they will have responsibility if they reach the main board. They may for example be given all the papers on some important issues and have to make a decision on them which is then presented to the main board. While some organizations have found this process successful, the only organization of which I have personal experience abandoned it after an experiment. It was found that dissatisfaction and frustration outweighted the contribution to managerial decision making or the learning by individual managers.

Learning from new jobs

Managers move into new jobs through different purposes and processes, singly or in combination. Chapter 7 shows that planned development was rarely an important cause or effect.

Moves can be analysed first according to type and then according to the content of the job involved in the move as follows:

Types of move
  Line promotion
  Job rotation/change of function
  Secondment
  'Assistant to'

Differences in content related to
  Geographical shift
  Product
  Organization culture
  Division or corporate experience

Any of these moves may be either within the manager's existing organization or to a new organization. The development experience involved was much more intense when a move involved going into a new organization. It was possible to see an ascending hierarchy of difficulty, relating both to the need to develop new managerial abilities and the problems involved in doing so.

The least complex process is that of moving up the existing line in the manager's current organization. This is not to imply that it is easy.

Next is the process when one 'constant' is retained. This may happen when a manager stays in the same organization but moves from one function to another, for example from marketing into personnel. It may occur when the function is the constant but the manager moves to another organization.

The third stage of difficulty is when a manager changes both basic function and level in an organization, for example being promoted from finance director to general manager.

The fourth level occurs when this functional and level change is accompanied by change in the organization in which the manager works (Figure 2.1).

FAMILIAR	Same function, same organization
PART FAMILIAR	Same function, different organization
	Different function, same organization
UNFAMILIAR	New job, new organization

Figure 2.1 Learning problems in job moves

In our survey we found people in each of these categories. In one organization for example we found that the shortest length of company service on the board of directors was 21 years, and the shortest length of service as a main board director 11 years. In effect they were all 'boy and man' members of the organization and had not experienced the delights or terrors of being exposed to the particular learning opportunities and problems of life outside their organization. On the other hand we went to another multinational organization in which only one of the seven main board directors we saw had substantial experience within that organization. (The experience the others had developed outside, as compared with insiders, was the reason why they had been recruited.)

Entry into a new job provided both a need for new areas of effectiveness for the manager concerned and the recognition that these new areas had to be learned. Again this was a recognition which our directors seemed to achieve more often after the event than before it. However, there were rather more frequent statements showing that they had recognized before entering such jobs that there was a learning experience involved. Indeed on some occasions this was the reason why the job was taken on. While generally we found an absence both organizationally and personally of a master plan for development, this does not necessarily mean that individuals faced with a particular job opportunity are not able to distinguish that there is a development and learning opportunity involved in it.

Line promotion

Movement up the line is described as the least complex development experience because the manager carries with him or her the comfort of knowing technically what the job is about. It was a commonplace observation among the directors that as they moved up a straight line the problems they were faced with and their learning needs related less to the technical content of the process they were managing and more to the managerial elements. They became exposed to a wider range of activities outside their immediate function on which they were expected to have a view and with which they were supposed to have an effective working relationship.

Whereas for example an area sales manager spends a lot of his time directly selling, and the rest of his time managing the work of his subordinates, the activities and priorities of a sales director would be quite different. The sales director would need an understanding of and ability to make a contribution on wider issues such as cash management and inventory control.

At each new stage in the line there are changed requirements for what the manager has to do, changed learning needs and also changed learning opportunities. If the manager has to respond to a wider range of influences, which increases his problems in managing, at least he has the opportunity to learn from them.

Most of the directors we saw felt that this kind of movement, although it involved stages in their learning process, was not the most difficult or illuminating of their career. It seems likely in fact that they may have understated the difficulty of these transitions. A few directors did identify important learning experience derived from a line promotion.

One described how he had moved from being the general manager of a company with 400 employees to take responsibility for a company in the same organization with three times that number of staff.

> I could not have done the second job as successfuly as I did without the first experience, but I had to learn a quite different kind of management style in the second job. In the first I knew most of the people and was always aware of what was going on. In the second job I really did have to manage through other people

and rely on them. In turn that job and that experience has made it possible for me to do my current job successfuly. I have companies all round the world and there is no way I could have moved from the ability to handle things directly, as I did in the first company mentioned, to my responsibilities here – or at least to do that successfully.

Job rotation/change of function

The majority of directors we saw had not acquired experience in the direct management of a number of individual functions, though they might have had general responsibility for several functions either before they went on the board or as a result of that appointment. The latter is however different from working directly as the accountable manager for a function. Job rotation may mean the collection of direct experience of managing different departments within one function, such as working in three departments of the finance function. It can also mean experience in several different functions, for example moving between production, marketing and product development. Some of our directors had engaged in this sort of move and had benefited from it. The benefits of such moves might indeed be experienced by the organization even if individuals stayed at middle management level, but the relevance of these moves in equipping people for the top was certainly recognized by many of the individuals to whom we spoke.

Although seen as desirable however, and rated highly by those who had been involved in it, the process created problems at both the personal and organizational level. The difficulties involved in the transition both for the manager involved and those around the manager were recognized. The individual had to struggle with different job content and to sustain credibility. The learning experiences were not fully recognized or managed.

There were dramatic examples of what was involved. 'I became Operations Director when I knew nothing about production; I had to learn or go under. I am sure I am a much better Managing Director because of this experience.'

Job rotation is highly valued in management development literature. The fact that we found relatively little evidence of it is supported by a survey published in 1984.[1] This showed that only 5 per cent of 50 companies routinely used cross posting between functions as an active form of management development. It is probable however that moves occurred which were not an 'active form of management development' in the sense of being planned and systematic. Given the difficulties involved in cross-functional moves this seems likely to be one of the areas in which the values of the formal management development system are in conflict with the realities of managerial life.

If wide-ranging experience in a number of functions is not apparently provided through job moves, the learning which it is desired to secure through such moves will not be acquired. If it is throught desirable to give managers experience of a range of functions, alternative processes – either on the job through projects and task forces or off the job through structured programmes – will need to be implemented.

Secondment

Some organizations saw the movement of an individual manager from his existing company or division to another company or division in the business as being a secondment. There were a few examples of this kind of substantial transfer, normally involving a manager moving from his existing role to the same or a similar role in another part of the organization. From a learning point of view what was involved was the change to a different kind of environment in perhaps a different country. More substantial learning opportunities were involved where the manager moved either into a different role in the business, which has similarities in effect to the job rotation process, or outside the organization.

In the United Kingdom secondments occur perhaps most frequently between commerce and industry and the civil service (and vice versa). They may also occur where a manager is sent to manage some worthy project outside the business on a temporary basis.

We encountered no directors who had had this sort of experience. The more pessimistic view of this would be that people who are going to get to the top are not seconded outside the business because it creates too much of an interruption in their career and does too little for them. The more optimistic view would be that the idea of secondment outside is relatively new and has had too little chance to work its way through to be demonstrated in people now at the top of our organizations. It certainly seems to imply a degree of planning and commitment on the part of both the individual and the organization which many of them would be reluctant to engage in. From a development point of view secondments also illustrate the higher levels of difficulty, since they often involve changes of role and by definition always involve moving into a strange culture.

'Assistant to'

There is one variant on the alternatives of job rotation and secondment, the 'assistant to' position. This is not a line promotion and does not involve overt authority over managers. It was for a time quite a popular device for exposing people to the realities of top management, giving an individual a view from the top while at the same time providing an often over-burdened top executive with someone who would take part of his burden. This process is still widely used in the civil service, where high-flyers are put through the Minister's private office as a matter of planned development. It seems to be rather less popular now in industry and commerce than it was perhaps 20 years ago. We encountered one or two individuals with this sort of experience. Although usually prepared to say that it had given them some relevant knowledge, they also said that operating in this role without direct accountability was not the best way of learning how to manage.

A rather more interesting variant had influenced the development of some of our respondents. While holding a direct job as subordinate to a managing director they had acquired informally some of the aspects of 'assistant to' by being asked to think about problems, look into certain issues and occasionally even represent the senior executive on visits or at meetings. While some of these activities were clearly rather similar to being given particular projects to do and indeed may have involved exactly that, there were occasions which involved a rather more substantial and more permanent relationship. What the manager learned would partly be a response to the content of the issues which he addressed, and partly a response to the particular relationship with the boss which we will be looking at in Chapter 4.

The content of new jobs

The most substantial difference in jobs occurs when there is a move between functions. Major development opportunities can also occur when the location of the job is changed.

Geographical shift

Several of our directors commented on the additional learning they had secured by working in companies outside the United Kingdom. Two different kinds of learning were involved. Firstly they encountered different ways of doing things which could be used to test and challenge the processes by which they had made their success so far. This kind of experience might be helpful in managing any of their jobs in the organization.

Secondly there were the even more significant opportunities of learning from different national cultures. The way in which these differences impinge on what the director does is covered in Chapter 10. The development experience was often perceived by those who had been involved as a turning point. One director told us that the experience of working in Japan for three years had totally transformed the way he saw his business and how he should manage it. A number of directors commented on the extent to which working away from the United Kingdom gave greater opportunities for autonomy, for operating without either central support or central intervention. They saw this process as a very important development experience both in its own right and for understanding how to operate yourself when you become the person at the centre who ought to provide relevant support and ought not to interfere.

Product

A number of directors had worked on different products, sometimes by moving between different organizations with different products and sometimes by moving between different product lines in one organization. Changes here could be very dramatic if the different organizations were as far apart as retail management and heavy engineering. The shift could also be quite significant within an organization. The problems for example of marketing chemicals used in cosmetics differ from those of marketing chemicals used in agriculture. Similarly a move between housing and civil engineering in a construction company would bring out significantly different issues of direction and management.

Organization culture

One of our directors had moved from an organization which he described as a brilliantly managed autocracy to another which he described as a chaotic democracy. At the time we saw him he was in a third organization which was attempting to change from being a conservative bureaucracy to an innovative organization based on consultation. The type of organization impacts directly on the job the manager does as described in Chapters 8 and 9. From a learning point of view experience in a wide range of organization cultures not only demands the ability to learn how to manage in each of them, it also brings the potential to learn how to manage better within each new experience by using what has been learned in the old – although part of that experience may not fit!

Division or corporate experience

Nearly all the directors we saw had experience in both the centre of the organization and in its subsidiary parts. Very few had only corporate experience. The divisional experience was sometimes but not always the same as 'profit centre' experience mentioned below. The value of having both kinds of experience on the way to the top was often expressed in very pragmatic terms. 'There is nothing that they can do, nothing they can try to hide, that I haven't done and hidden before them when I worked in a division.' The experience of our directors sometimes involved three moves; they may have started in the centre, gone out to a division and then come back into the centre for their final main board job.

Profit centre experience

Some directors worked in organizations, perhaps of very substantial size, whose main board was the only place where accountability for revenue and expenditure was drawn together. Others worked (or had worked) in organizations where subsidiary companies or divisions held responsibility as 'profit centres', with very substantial, if not full, accountability for all expenditure and income.

Where however directors arrived at the main board without ever having operated in a subsidiary profit centre, let alone as the manager of a profit centre, the transition was a difficult one. Obviously enough this situation tended to occur in highly centralized organizations with strong functional lines. In these situations managers could arrive at the top having managed very successfully in a relatively narrow domain. Where on the other hand they had been involved in and perhaps managed a profit centre, involving the collection of all the functional elements under one accountability, perhaps under one roof, their on-the-job learning would be much enhanced.

Experiences outside the organization

Relatively few directors quoted significant outside experience. The examples here are those directly connected to the manager's job. (Illustrations or other kinds of experience outside are given in Chapter 5.)

The closest relationship in job experience occurs with involvement on external bodies such as industrial committees, professional institutions and governmental review bodies. Sometimes the activities are local, such as participating in a county committee concerned with Industry Year. Sometimes it is a national event; we interviewed one director who had headed a national investigation as a result of which the committee was actually known by his name.

Most of these external activities were taken up because the organization needed a representative on a committee, or wanted to be involved in a particular investigation in order to influence it. Although naturally enough never referring to themselves, some directors murmured gently about 'people I have known' who had got engaged in external activities more for reasons of personal prestige than for any return to the organization. Most directors, if they had such external experiencies, did not rate them at all significantly as learning processes, and indeed they were often puzzled by the thought that they could be so described. A few had picked up direct learning, for example by being exposed to different kinds of membership on a committee, or being involved with the civil service for the first time. 'A lot of our business is affected by government decisions one way or another, whether Tory or Labour. My first experience of being exposed both to civil servants and then finally to the Minister himself was very important in terms of helping us to see how to make the approach in the right way, ie how to make the case they were interested in rather than the case which we might have wanted to make.'

We encountered one director who had explicitly sought a position on a committee in order to develop his own skills as a manager. He was a general manager with an extensive financial background, who secured nomination to an important industry committee on another functional subject in which he was interested.

Stages of learning in a new job

The difficulty of the learning process is related to the type of novelty involved in a new job. The following comments were drawn from our interviews and from my own experience of work in industry and commerce. Our discussions did not cover the duration of the learning process in a new job. Indeed, since the nature of the challenge is different the length of time will also differ. A valuable contribution on the general question of length, and particularly on the kind of learning involved at different stages of adaptation to a new job, is presented by other researchers. Jennings,[2] in one of the early studies of managerial jobs and career development, claimed that most jobs could be mastered within 12–18 months. More recent and better based research, particularly addressed to the highest level of management, offers a different view. The most specific study is that of John Gabarro,[3] who identifies different stages in taking charge of a new general management job, and different learning within those stages. While he emphasizes that there will be differences between individuals and their reactions to different situations he identifies five predictable stages:

Taking hold
Immersion
Reshaping
Consolidation
Refinement

The *taking hold stage* typically lasts three–six months. He quotes a manager: 'You have to learn the product, people and the problem. You're trying like hell to learn about the organization and the people awfully fast and that's the trickiest thing. At first you're afraid to do anything for fear of upsetting the applecart. The problem is that you have to keep the business running while you are learning about it.' At this stage the manager is grappling with the nature of the new situation, understanding tasks and problems and assessing the organization and its requirements.

At the *immersion stage* learning is more focused on particular interaction and conflict, asking more specific questions and looking at reactions to changes already introduced. This lasts 4–11 months.

At *the reshaping stage* there is less 'new' learning and probably more confirming information.

At *the consolidation stage* learning involves two sets of issues. It is necessary to identify problems associated with previous action and there is more likely to be an attempt to diagnose and solve unanticipated problems. Learning also continues from actions undertaken in the earlier stages.

The refinement stage of learning in the new job, which probably no longer feels very new, involves looking for new opportunities. Learning is more incremental and routine unless interventions occur from outside; but that is nothing to do with the newness of the job. Gabarro says that learning is deepest at the immersion and consolidation stages. This is probably because he emphasizes the reflective aspect of learning which is strongest at this stage.

The view that learning from a new job is a substantial and relatively lengthy process is supported also by the research done by Kotter.[4] Kotter's study supports the view presented earlier that there are particular difficulties for managers moving into new jobs. The most successful managers in his study of general managers had spent most of their time in the industry in which they were now working, and indeed 81 per cent had spent their career entirely with their present employers. The reasons for this relationship are discussed in Chapter 8 where we look at what general managers actually have to do. The relationship to the learning process is that managers have to spend time in a new job on developing agendas for their businesses and developing networks of resources needed to accomplish these agendas. These are not processes responsive to a quick fix.

Converting opportunities into learning

So far the analysis has shown a wide number of situations in which jobs provide learning opportunities, and some of the ways in which these opportunities have been taken up. It was clear from our discussions that there was little awareness of these opportunities beforehand, and action was rarely taken to turn them into effective learning. The basic reason was an inherent tendency to see the immediate task purposes within the jobs as the prime issue. The directors had not recognized at the time in many cases, and may have recognized subsequently only through our questions, the actualities of learning or development associated with the tasks.

We are faced with the fundamental paradox that doing the job effectively is the core, the central purpose, of a manager's life, while learning from actually carrying out managerial activities is widely experienced as the most relevant process; yet the emphasis on successful task completion has not been properly balanced by successful use of the learning opportunity. Part of the reason is undoubtedly a general unawareness of learning opportunities. We also found that attempts to plan some aspects of the provision of development opportunities had not worked out as well as management development specialists might have hoped. While managers might not be very good at recognizing all the opportunities within jobs, at least the provision, for example, of planned job moves generates opportunities from which managers will undoubtedly learn. Yet even in those organizations which attempt this sort of process, the feedback to us was that such interventions in careers were perceived by the recipients as much less powerful and influential than the organization thought. This comment is amplified in Chapter 7.

In summary therefore the experience of most of the directors we saw of learning from the job had been what we call 'Type 1 Management Development'. This is summarized in Figure 2.2.

While discussions with us showed this sort of accidental and insufficient picture, they also showed that directors were partly aware that learning on the job could be a better managed experience. They felt that learning opportunities for example from a particular project or from a new job could have been spelled out beforehand, and that this would have increased the chance of learning from it. What is required is a better marriage between the process of managing and the process of learning from managing. A

Type 1 'Informal managerial' – accidental processes

Characteristics	– occur within managerial activities – explicit intention is task performance – no clear development objectives – unstructured in development terms – not planned in advance – owned by managers
Development consequences	– learning is real, direct, unconscious, insufficient

Figure 2.2 Type 1 Management Development

marriage will be successful only if it is understood that the manager's prime concern is with the process of managing and that learning will be a subsidiary purpose. A manager wants to be effective; he does not want to be a learner. He may accept being a learner for some of the time, for some processes, in order to become effective. To some extent the people we interviewed believed that this had happened, but they had begun to recognize that the relationship could have been clarified and thereby improved.

The combination of learning and doing

The most frequently quoted circumstance in which learning from managing occurred was that of actually tackling a problem. A manager had as part of his normal work, or was given by his boss, a particular problem to resolve. The manager collected information about it, probably discussed it with colleagues, perhaps tested out alternative solutions on them. He would go back to his boss and discuss alternatives, make a recommendation or communicate to him the decision which he had already made.

The decision would have consequences. At the point of recommending action to his boss, or at the subsequent point of reviewing the success or failure of the decision, the manager would experience the consequences. If the recommendation was faulty because he presented it badly, had failed to review sufficient alternatives, or had not worked out the negative as well as the positive consequences, comments would follow. At all these stages and in different ways the problem-solving process was a learning experience. Most particularly, as suggested earlier, the consequences of a decision would also provide learning.

It was quite clear from our respondents that by far the greatest element in their development was this sort of process. It was carried out over a large variety of activities hour by hour and day by day. Sometimes it was explicit and well done and sometimes inexplicit and badly done. This is what managers mean by 'learning by experience'.

The review process could be more efficient and effective at both task and learning levels. An illustration of how such a process works is shown in Figure 2.3.

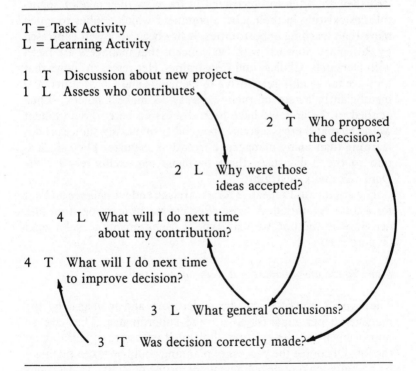

T = Task Activity
L = Learning Activity

1 T Discussion about new project
1 L Assess who contributes

2 T Who proposed the decision?

2 L Why were those ideas accepted?

4 L What will I do next time about my contribution?

4 T What will I do next time to improve decision?

3 L What general conclusions?

3 T Was decision correctly made?

Figure 2.3 Learning cycle, combining task and learning

Using reality

The proposition developed in this chapter has been that the process of learning from jobs could be made quicker and more effective if the opportunities and processes involved were better understood. The argument that learning on the job is a natural way of learning is correct as far as it goes, but incorrect in that it tends to assume that no deliberate action is necessary to improve the 'natural' behaviour. Learning from the job offers the greatest increase in learning productivity simply because the opportunities are so frequent and varied in comparison with alternative processes for learning, such as courses which are infrequent and often, in some respects, irrelevant.

To obtain the productivity, managers need to recognize that the opportunities are there. One of the problems faced by managers is that they are often too restricted in the view they take of opportunities existing in their jobs, a comment which applies to much more than learning opportunities. It has been very well expressed by Rosemary Stewart[5] with her concept that managers are faced with Demands, Choices and Constraints. Her research shows that they are too readily responsive to Demands and Constraints, and insufficiently aware of their capacity to make Choices. When applied to the area we have been discussing here, the argument would be that there is a greater possibility of making choices about learning than many managers currently recognize. Their dedication to the task causes them to focus too exclusively on the Demands and Constraints.

The argument, I repeat, is for a marriage and for balance and not for a total revolution. A more effective use of learning from task activities is the one we call Type 2 Management Development (Figure 2.4).

Planning the use of managerial work for development

The Type 2 processes can be undertaken and managed by the managerial participants, bosses and subordinates. They are an improvement on the existing unplanned processes of learning on the job. Of course the process of planning could be taken further – by actually making development the prime objective in decisions about jobs, projects and managerial activities. Very little of this had

Type 2 'Integrated managerial' – opportunistic processes

Characteristics	– occur within managerial activities
	– explicit intention both task performance and development
	– clear development objectives
	– structured for development by boss and subordinate
	– planned beforehand or reviewed subsequently as learning experiences
	– owned by managers
Development consequences	– learning is real, direct, conscious, more substantial

Figure 2.4 Type 2 Management Development

occurred with directors in our survey; ways in which such formal management development processes can be designed and managed are described in Chapter 7.

Summary

Learning from experience is felt by managers to be the most frequent and often the most influential feature in their development. Learning from a new task or new job presents both the biggest opportunity and most severe challenge, but most opportunities occur within the existing job.

While directors had 'learned from experience', many of them now recognized that they learned less, and less well, than they might have done. The prime causes of this were a failure to recognize beforehand the opportunities created by job experiences, and a failure to review after an experience what had been learned from it. The accidental, informal and inefficient experiences described here as Type 1 can be converted into Type 2 Management Development, adding learning more effectively to the achievement of managerial tasks.

References

1   Egon Zehnder International, *Management Resources,* Egon Zehnder, London, June, 1984
2   Jennings, E., *The Middle Manager,* University of Michigan, Michigan, 1967
3   Gabarro, J., 'When a new manager takes charge', *Harvard Business Review,* May–June 1985
4   Kotter, J.P., *The General Managers,* Free Press, New York, 1982
5   Stewart, R., *Choices for the Manager,* McGraw-Hill, Maidenhead, 1982

3 Learning from other managers: how

I started to write this chapter on Thanksgiving Day. This reminded me that Christopher Columbus, normally credited with the discovery of what became the United States, in fact set out from Spain with quite a different purpose. He set out not to discover the New World, which indeed he did not know was there, but to find a sea passage round the Old World.

We have already seen that much the same phenomenon happens in learning from the job, namely that managers while pursuing the task learn from doing so, but that most often learning is both incidental and accidental. If however this is true of the way in which an individual solitarily learns from doing the job, it does not follow that it is also true for those processes of learning which while still centred on the job are more often shared. The contribution of other people might be better organized, more frequently directed explicitly with a learning objective, and more intensively experienced as learning rather than task completion. Our survey gave us the chance to test the extent to which learning from other managers was a more directed and effective process.

We did not think it likely in advance that learning from other managers in the context of the job would be a highly programmed and efficient process. We did not assume that it would be like a well-organized training course, complete with objectives, appropriate choice of methods, opportunity to experiment and provision for reinforcement. Pascale and Athos[1] say about learning:

41

You do not learn to wage war by studying a manual. You do not become an artist by painting someone else's dots. There are some complex human activities, and management is one of them, in which it is the aesthetic fit, ie the form and harmony of things, that matters most. Division and sub-division of tasks and intellectualising and verbalising will never accomplish the learning that experiencing, watching, feeling, sensing and imitating will.

Chapters 5 and 6 look at ways in which complex managerial skills may be broken down and perhaps developed through a formal, designed training process. This chapter and the next describe less well-organized learning derived from working with other people. The learning occurs through the interaction of

> particular kinds of learning process, eg coaching, observing
> particular relationships, with boss, peers, mentors
> stages in the learning process

The complete interaction is shown in Figure 3.1.

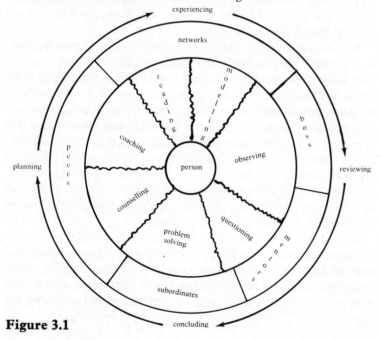

Figure 3.1

Any of the people indicated in the model may originate the learning opportunity. Bosses undoubtedly provide potentially the widest range of learning processes. They may provide coaching, counselling and actually be the model, and would certainly be involved in the problem-solving process. A manager's peers may perform the same functions. This chapter looks at the processes, the next at the people who may be offering the processes.

Coaching

Very few directors could recall any experience of being coached directly, in the sense of a boss or colleague taking them through a management process with the explicit intention of guiding them to better performance. Certainly the attention devoted in the literature to coaching as a necessary and desirable process had not impinged on the working life of the people we saw.

One of the few illustrations of coaching concerned a director who had been responsible for one of two major products in a company but knew nothing of the other. His boss, who was also responsible for the second product line, brought him in for individual discussions about the development of a new project on this second line. 'Just the two of us. He took me through all the steps involved, the papers, the snags. He was explicit about it – he was teaching me the side of the business I did not know.'

The lack of coaching was partly explained by the prevalence of the shared problem-solving discussed below. Explicit coaching was rare; picking up learning from the discussion of problems in a task-centred way was not.

Counselling

We used this term to describe the process by which a manager is given general guidance on issues requiring his or her attention as a manger. The issues might be specific, as in: 'The way you put your quesion makes it sound like an interrogation rather than a shared search for truth.' It might be general: 'You need to work on your relationships with other people.' This type of feedback, relating to performance in the current job, is a familiar part of the managerial scene. There is also general career guidance in the sense of managers being counselled to aim themselves towards a particular job, or indeed away from a particular job or career destination. We used the word 'counselling' in order to embrace the informal and accidental processes as well as the structured experiences provided by the formal processes of performance or potential review often called appraisal.

While a large number of directors had been in organizations where appraisal systems had been in operation for many years, they had not apparently been powerful and useful experiences, at least from a development point of view. A few directors could remember helpful activities resulting from this formal process and a few could remember being affected by informal and unstructured feedback which helped them to change their behaviour or to aim in a particular direction in their career.

In terms of interventions from outside, therefore, those which would have been the most powerful coaching and counselling, seem to have been largely absent.

Modelling

A few directors said they had studied how an admired performer achieved his managerial ends. 'I watched him and saw how he rewarded people.' 'When we had a problem he always went round the table first, with no indication of his own ideas. I saw he got more and better ideas that way than I did by stating my views first, so I changed.'

Some directors learned how not to do things. 'He was devious and people knew it. I decided not to be like him.' Examples of this kind perhaps justify a separate section called 'Anti-modelling'!

Iacocca[2] quotes how he learned from the experience of Knudsen, brought in as President of Ford from General Motors. He did not bring any General Motors executive with him. 'Nobody at Ford felt much loyalty to Knudsen, so he was without a power base. As a result, he found himself alone in an alien atmosphere, never really accepted. A decade later when I went to Chrysler, I made sure not to repeat that mistake.'

We were surprised by the very low level of response to the question on modelling. Perhaps one answer was given by the directors themselves. Many of them said that modelling was something they believed 'must have happened' but which was unconscious. By this they obviously meant that it was not only unplanned but also that they had incorporated the behaviour without fully assessing the reason. Their responses on this, indeed, are interestingly different from their responses in many other fields of learning. Elsewhere, although not recognizing the learning at the time, they were able to recall subsequently in some detail what they had learned. In this particular area they were not able to do so.

This suggests that modelling is an area in which we should be even more wary than others in making predictions about what will happen or assertions about what has happened. We should certainly remember that very few managers have been trained in the techniques of behaviour analysis, and that they are probably not well equipped to analyse the particulars of behaviour.

It seems likely that modelling is going on which is not only often unconscious but also probably varies between individuals. As in many aspects of learning, some people are probably better equipped to learn from modelling than are others. Indeed it is likely that some individuals learn differently from the same process. One manager may observe, reflect and act, while another many observe and incorporate quickly with relatively little thought.

The consequence of relatively unconscious modelling could be that a particular form of behaviour is taken up and used in different, less appropriate circumstances. We encountered an example of this from a director who said that he had seen how effective another manager was in using a highly structured control process over a meeting, intended to ensure that objectives were met and that the time scales for the meeting were achieved. When, however, he moved to a different division in his organization and continued to run meetings in this way, he found that this style did not fit the purpose of meetings which were intended to be creative and ideas-producing. 'It took me much longer than it should have done because of my past experience of success in the original style to realize that I needed to encourage free flow, if ideas were to come through and be developed.'

Finally, perhaps an important corrective statement about the whole process of modelling was given by Sir Alec Guinness in his autobiography, where he attributes to Dr Johnson the following: 'Almost all absurdity of conduct arises from the imitation of those we cannot resemble.'

Asking questions

Arjay Miller was an experienced manager who worked with the young Henry Ford II. He thought Ford was a good learner. 'He did not try to conceal his ignorance,' remembers Miller, 'he knew what he didn't know. He was never afraid to ask questions.'[3]

It is perhaps not surprising that, in the absence of the kind of direct inputs which might have been made through coaching and counselling, at the instigation of someone else, much more learning is secured by the manager's own initiative. Particularly when managers go into a new job, the process of asking questions in order to obtain both direct knowledge and what they will often call the 'feel' of the situation is of prime importance. Indeed, since the job of a manager can be seen in one sense as being largely about the securing and manipulating of information, the process of learning by asking questions is a contantly recurring one. It is not one which directors themselves often identified, probably because it seems so natural to them. The process of acquiring information strikes them as managerial, ie a necessary task rather than a learning process. 'Why did that happen?' 'What do the figures say on that point?' 'Has James ever worked on that kind of project before?' 'What percentage of our business to our three biggest customers represent?'

In view of the examples just given it is important to emphasize the double-sided nature of the learning secured from asking such questions. There is the overt objective normally linked with the direct managerial processes and seen as such by those involved. There is also very often the secondary objective of testing out and better understanding the giver of the information. From these sorts of question therefore managers not only learn the factual information they need in order to do their job but also develop opinions about the people involved, the nature of the situation, aspects which may not be overt parts of their objective in asking the questions but which subsequently provide a large part of the benefit.

Observing

A large part of the modelling process derives from observing others in action. The observation and the observer's action derived from it are linked, although probably often unconsciously. Obervation also exists independent of the modelling process. Like question asking it is a process by which information is acquired. It is information about the behaviour of other people, about interactions between people and departments, about the way things are done. 'I visited factories in three different countries. I found the blue collar workers were not actually working harder; it is not that our people on the shop floor are lazy it is that in the other countries they were much better organized for work.' The same manager with production experience went out on a visit to a series of customers with his sales director. 'As the production director I was usually annoyed when the sales people came in with some complaint or request that affected me. Just one day visiting the customer showed me more about both the reality of the way our products were put to use and the kind of very reasonable issues that were raised with my sales colleague.'

Problem-solving

The basic process of problem-solving was described in the previous chapter as an illustration of the job-centred processes of learning. In that example the process was described as one-to-one interaction between a manager and a boss, with some discussion perhaps with colleagues. This kind of process happened also with a much stronger and more continuous involvement of other managers.

A problem might occur during the day – perhaps a major customer was threatening to withdraw an order unless certain actions were taken such as granting a higher discount. So an informal ad hoc group of managers would be drawn together, and perhaps indeed would grow during the process of discussions. The task focus would be 'what do we do?'

A learning experience might occur, for example, for a marketing manager faced with the alternative arguments of the production director and the finance director. The production director might be relatively happy to let the order go on the grounds that it was difficult to complete anyway. The finance director's view might be more focused on the potential impact on cash flow. The sales director might be drawn into the picture because he might be bothered about the precedent involved, but also he might be concerned about the impact on total sales volume and therefore perhaps even on his personal incentive payment.

Managers had learned from this kind of experience in many different ways. They learned about the reality of how decisions were made and perhaps about good and bad ways of reaching decisions. Problems of this kind also tend to bring to the surface many issues about priorities in different departments, anxieties and urgencies often otherwise concealed under urbane monthly presentations at management meetings.

While ad hoc meetings of this kind are a very frequent occurrence, equally significant from a learning point of view can be meetings often planned well in advance perhaps with detailed and carefully organized presentations and papers. The meetings might be about the development of a corporate plan or business strategy.

> I remember my first experience in this organization of being involved in discussions about whether we should extend our operations into a country we had never worked in before. We started with big figures about all the markets we weren't in, and then we looked at the problems involved. I was very enthusiastic about going to a particular country, but then one of my colleagues went over his experience of working there for another organization. It was like having a tutorial about the realities of managing abroad.

As with the process of asking questions, this process of problem-solving contained different types of learning. First, as the last example shows, knowledge is acquired at two levels – facts on a particular case, and knowledge necessary to resolve similar issues

It involves also learning from the process, in the sense of how the problem is attacked.

> Our planning people used to produce huge volumes of documents for this big meeting once a year. Because they presumed quite rightly that most people would not read them, the first two or three hours were spent with them giving us presentations repeating essentially the same information. I suffered and learned and proposed how we should do it differently.

The third kind of learning is again that of learning from and about the people involved, of how or whether they present themselves, their departments and the situation they are trying to describe effectively.

A particular activity within the problem-solving process is of special interest.

> We had a difficult problem to negotiate with another division in the company. I had been working on this with some colleagues, and we went into my boss with our proposed answer. I was a few sentences into my explanation of our proposal when he told me he had read the paper from which I was speaking. 'You don't need to convince me; we have to convince him. I'll be Jack Green, now you set about convincing me.' So I was into a role play.

The director involved then went on to describe how, during the interaction between himself and his boss, they had improved their actual presentation, and how much he had learned from the process on trying to influence someone to your point of view.

Problem-solving, covering a tremendous range of activities of which only a tiny number are illustrated here, provides an additional explanation as to why coaching and counselling were rarely identified. It is not only that they are found to be uncomfortable by managers who are not trained in them. They are also not seen as priority managerial activities. Problem-solving, however, is perhaps the central managerial activity. Many directors who told us they had never been coached were able to give illustrations of how the problem-solving process had in effect provided something of the same kind of learning experience. Managers learn from the experience of being exposed to problems, of sharing analysis, discussion and eventual implementation with colleagues and bosses. They were not taken through the problems with a development objective and therefore were not coached in the formal sense. They were guided managerially, both explicitly and indirectly, by others involved and learned from this process. As in many other areas in our discussions, directors were able to see after the event that this, the most real of processes for many of them, could be perceived more clearly as a learning process, organized better for it, with the consequence of a more productive total process.

Reading

All of the processes of learning from others mentioned so far involve some direct contact with other managers. Reading is different because it is a solitary process. Further comment about reading appears in later chapters. This section concentrates on those aspects of reading which explicitly derive from either other managers in the organization or from managerial authors outside it. It also suggests how reading as a solitary learning process is converted or supplemented as a result of discussing the material with other people.

Most of our managers spend a great deal of their time reading, but the vast proportion of this was reading related directly to their responsibilities at work. They read reports, they read financial statements, they read memos and letters. At the simplest level of acquiring knowledge, they learned from other managers in the organization both facts and opinions. They also learned, as illustrated earlier on other processes, about the individuals who were writing the memos and letters. They learned about their competence, their interests, their understanding of difficult issues.

As with other processes, reading adds both to the store of knowledge and to understanding about that knowledge. 'I did not know we had a big problem of any kind until I saw the first letter. I didn't know we had a big problem until I saw the responses of all my colleagues to it.'

In one organization in which I worked several directors confessed that they were unable to understand the reports being issued by the Research Department. As a result two different reports were published. The Research Department continued to write their necessarily extremely complex and technical documents. In addition they produced a special version which was not a summary of the complex technical document but a report which brought out those issues of concern to non-technical directors. Whereas they had been unable to understand and therefore had learned nothing, now they could learn and indeed began to ask questions which were not merely intelligent but important.

The vast volume of written material that directors read is almost entirely devoted to task effectiveness. They read in order to get their jobs done better. Most of the people we saw read very little about management in general. However, as it happened we struck them at a time when the massive best-seller by Lee Iacocca was most visible. Amongst those people who read anything, Iacocca's book[2] was frequently mentioned. What such books have to say that may be of value to managers is discussed in later chapters. Here it is only necessary to say that reading of this kind is still a minority pursuit. Interestingly it remains also a solitary pursuit. The Iacocca book and articles in, for example, the *Harvard Business Review* by respectable management practitioners seem to be read almost secretly by individuals. There was remarkably little evidence of sharing any conclusions derived from this kind of reading. Perhaps directors were frightened of acquiring the reputation of being intellectual, which is of course fatal in most organizations. Whatever the reason there seemed a substantial loss of opportunity. The individual could gain much more from such reading, by discussing it with colleagues. This kind of process is one of the virtues of reading in association with a formal training programme. We found a few examples where directors exchanged opinions with similarly minded colleagues, but none where this process was well organized.

Reading therefore from a learning point of view seems to present opportunities not fully seized by many. There are good articles and books by thoughtful management practitioners which would at least help managers to consider alternatives to their present process, and might in many cases help them to avoid unnecessary mistakes. Even managers who read books fail to get the full benefit from reading.

CONTENT KNOWLEDGE OR UNDERSTANDING
    About the immediate managerial activity
    About the relationship of specific activity to other kinds of
    activity
PROCESS UNDERSTANDING
    About the ways issues can be managed
INTERPERSONAL UNDERSTANDING
    About people involved
    About skills used

Figure 3.2   Some types of learning

Summary

This chapter examined how managers learn from each other. It shows particularly how managers learn from their own awareness of what they and others do as managers. The formal management development processes of coaching and counselling have in contrast been seen to be less frequently available or effective.

The different types of learning are summarized in Figure 3.2.

References

1 Pascale, R.T. and Athos, A.G., *The Art of Japanese Management*, Penguin Books, London 1982
2 Iacocca, L., *Iacocca*, Sidgwick & Jackson, London, 1985
3 Lacey, R., *Ford*, Heinemann, London, 1986

4 Learning from other managers: who

We now divert our attention from the process used to the person offering the help. As indicated in Figure 3.1, any of the processes mentioned there might be offered by any of the managerial contacts mentioned in this chapter. The likelihood of a particular individual offering one of the processes, however, varies. For example, the boss would have a stronger likelihood of operating in the coaching mode (perhaps within the problem-solving approach) with a subordinate than would a subordinate with him!

Boss

Participants in our survey were asked to comment on the role of their bosses in two different ways. They were asked directly whether their bosses had had a significant influence on their development, and they were also asked about the kind of development activities their bosses engaged in, such as coaching, counselling and modelling.

There was a low level of response to both kinds of question. Since the role of the boss has always been seen in management development literature as a prime factor, we increased our questioning in this area to ensure that we were not being misled by superficial comments; but it made no difference to the level of response.

For some individual directors the role of a single boss or several bosses over a period of time had been fundamental to their development. 'I admired my first boss very much. He wasn't a leader in the conventional sense at all. He was dogged and determined and I learned a great deal from him. He advised me "whenever you take a decision, analyse it as much as time allows. Once you have taken a decision never wonder for an instant what would have happened if . . ." This advice was very sound and made me decisive.' 'My boss saw abilities in me way beyond those which I recognized in myself – he would set up a challenge which I constantly wanted to meet – then he would throw out another.' 'One of the reasons I resigned from X was a continually reducing level of respect for my bosses. Since then I have had very high regard for my bosses, they have all challenged me and made me stretch myself.'

One of the significant facts seems to be that most people quoted an early boss rather than later one. 'One of my early bosses made me swim managerially. He pushed me in but I knew he wouldn't let me drown.'

Different bosses sometimes provide different kinds of development in the career of a manager. 'One boss taught me how to prepare a case, because nothing got past him unless every dot and comma checked out. Another boss later taught me that you could ask for a clear case, yet show trust in the guy who was delivering it instead of distrust.'

Iacocca quotes the kind of intervention that a boss can make which is extremely important to both managerial effectiveness and to learning. ' "You want to do everything yourself. You don't know how to delegate." He taught me to stop trying to do everybody's job. "You're the best guy I've got, maybe as good as two guys put together. But you've got a hundred people working for you." ' He also quoted an experience of being coached by Robert MacNamara, later famous as Defence Secretary of the United States. ' "You are so effective one to one. You could sell anybody anything. But we are about to spend $100 million. Go home tonight and put your great idea on paper. If you can't do that you haven't really thought it out." It was a valuable lesson and I have followed his lead ever since.'

Our discussions showed that bosses made a much smaller contribution to formal processes such as coaching, counselling and discussing the purpose of job assignment than management development literature would suggest. Even their influence through informal processes – taking people through problem-solving or strategic thinking – was relatively small.

Since the role of the boss is quite rightly often identified as crucial it is worth discussing what seems not to have happened often with the people we saw. As a result of this more recent work I have amended slightly the views I published in 1984.[1] The boss has a set of roles related to the formal management development system:

Appraisal of performance
Appraisal of potential
Analysis of development needs and goals
Recognizing opportunities for learning (eg courses, projects)
Facilitating those opportunities for learning
Giving learning a priority

In addition the boss has a personal role embracing particularly the use of real management activities as learning opportunities:

Establishing learning goals
Accepting risks in subordinate performance
Monitoring learning achievement
Providing feedback on performance
Acting as a model of managerial behaviour
Acting as a model of learning behaviour
Understanding the learning styles of himself and others
Offering help
Providing direct coaching

One significant change from my 1984 list is that I have removed reference to the boss as mentor, which now seems to me a confusion of roles. It is more useful to regard the mentor as someone who does not have a direct line responsibility, as discussed later. (One of the best ways in which a boss can help others learn is of course to show a commitment to his own personal learning.)

Those bosses who had been most helpful to the people we interviewed had done some or all of the following:

Identified a managerial activity as a learning opportunity even though they might not always have made this explicit to the 'learner'

Discussed what the 'learner' had actually learned from the experience

Provided good explicit feedback about managerial action

Provided explicit suggestions for improvement

Taken some risks in placing managers in new jobs or on difficult projects or giving them more responsibility

These factors, as we found, are relatively rare. Given all the complexities and perceived higher priorities in boss/subordinate relationships this is not surprising. The relationship is often fraught not only because of differences in personal style but because of differences in priorities and values. In learning terms the boss/subordinate relationship was rarely highlighted. Such influence as there was may well have been buried under what were perceived by the interviewees to be much more significant issues about the relationship. A very interesting article by Gabarro and Kotter[2] shows the kind of demands necessary to establish an effective overall working relationship, but significantly does not refer at all to how subordinates might learn from their bosses.

Our survey did not fully reveal issues about men working for women. Whereas the women directors had all worked for male bosses, only one male director mentioned that he had learned from a female boss – and that was his very first appointment. The absence of female senior role models for women has frequently been identified as a problem for women managers. The lack of male experience in learning from a woman manager may also create both opportunities and problems as the number of female managers grows.

The boss/subordinate relationship is undeniably a powerful aid to learning; but in the real world job performance is the prime priority. Relationships between boss and subordinate are then complicated beyond the overall performance requirement by a wide range of other issues. The interpolation of a learning relationship is one which meets every demand of logic but immediately hits problems of application. Simplistic propositions that bosses should do more appraisal, more coaching, more counselling are particularly likely to fall on stony ground because the latter are seen as management development processes outside the range of real managerial priorities. Managers are more likely to add an element of learning to an existing managerial activity. Formal processes and purely activity centred learning are both needed, but informal processes will suit more managers and more situations.

Mentor

In our survey we used the word mentor to describe relationships
with people other than the boss. Essentially all the things which
bosses do for their subordinates are done as bosses and not as mentors. They may go to a lot of trouble to enhance the career prospects
of their subordinates, and it is easy to see why in consequence their
relationship has been described as a 'mentoring' one. From both a
practical point of view and most specifically from a learning point
of view, however, it is helpful to look at the role of the mentor as
being outside that of the boss. The contribution of the mentor proper, is often significantly different in terms of relationship. This
section therefore discusses the role of mentors as people who are
not direct bosses, although they may be managers on the next line
above, ie 'grandfathers'.

Mentoring covers relationships such as role model, guide, tutor,
coach, confidant and sponsor. In our survey we emphasized two different kinds of mentor. The first we saw as someone who offered a
direct relationship in which personal advice was given. The second
role was that of door-opener, who identified career possibilities,
and tried to make sure that someone for whom he had no direct line
responsibility was considered for the opportunity involved.

We found a few dramatic cases where directors recognized the
contribution made to their development by a mentor. Sometimes
an early boss became a later mentor. Overall, however, this was not
a process which the majority of directors believed they had
experienced.

It is relatively easy to explain the unawareness of the 'door opening' mentor. No doubt such processes are often carried on by informal exchanges between the senior managers about the capacities of
X or the desirability of Y doing a particular job. Comments made by
a mentor may be quite distant from any action taken but part of a
longer term process of making relevant people aware of the competence of an individual or of a desirable move for his development.
It may be that the mentor's contribution is not recognized because
the boss of the person under discussion feels that he has had the
most important influence on the person working for him. The personnel department might also make that claim. The actual contribution of the mentor might therefore be the subject of argument,
and the individuals could not know exactly what kind of approaches

were being made by a mentor even if they believed they actually had one.

The lack of comment on the more personal contribution that a mentor might have made is more difficult to explain. Perhaps directors were unwilling to attribute their success to any agency other than their own skills. However, some directors who claimed they had never had a mentor were quite prepared to say that they had been influenced by some external agency. Indeed we encountered several directors who mentioned individuals who claimed to be their mentors, but whom they had not experienced as such. As one director said, 'He constantly claimed that he was my mentor, and that he had not only given me opportunities, but had counselled me on my development. Possibly he did help with the oportunities, but we never had a serious discussion about what I did and how I did it in all the years I worked below him.'

Mentoring, if it existed at all, was an informal process. None of the directors had been exposed to a formal mentoring process of the kind described by Clutterbuck[3]; several organizations and directors, however, mentioned that mentoring as a formal process was part of their management development armoury now.

We encountered a few directors who made significant use of a personal contact outside the business. In two cases the contact had been a mentor of the director in a previous organization, and that relationship was sustained as their paths diverged. In both cases there was discussion not only about career plans but also particular problems and opportunities. The former can take place more comfortably with an outsider whereas the latter can often be done with colleagues, though there are circumstances in which this is not feasible.

The relatively low number of references to mentoring as an influencing process was a surprise in terms of its prominence in management development literature. There are however sufficient numbers of attested cases to show that it has been influential elsewhere. Bennis in his research on leaders,[4] for example, said that 'most were able to identify a small number of mentors and key experiences that powerfully shaped their philosophies, personalities and operating styles'. It is true that our survey shows differences not only on this question but also concerning his statement that 'leaders are perpetual learners, nearly all are highly proficient at learning from experience'. He says they were voracious readers and many learned from other people. The differences in our findings in other directions certainly justify caution about accepting his view about the significance of mentors. We are left with particular anecdotes from individuals. In his book Iacocca describes what was clearly a mentoring relationship with Charlie Beacham.

Perhaps one of the reasons why more mentoring is reported elsewhere than we found is precisely because of our distinction between the role of boss and that of a mentor. A number of the studies clearly describe boss activities as those of a mentor. About two-thirds of the 1250 executives in a survey by Roche[5] said they had a mentor or sponsor, but direct bosses were included as mentors.

There is no agreement on the correct word to describe the people the mentor is looking after: are they to be called protégés or mentees? The word protégé was certainly applied in one of the best known cases from the world of politics, that of Hugh Dalton the Labour politician. A biography of Dalton[6] lists the well-known politicians who had this relationship with him, including Hugh Gaitskell, and says that 'to these and others Dalton gave friendship, advice and practical assistance, channelling them to appropriate posts and on to appropriate committees and finding them candidatures. In return they fed him with new ideas and kept him entertained.' This brings out very well the fact that the relationship can be two-way. In Dalton's case the reference to new ideas suggests that it can be a shared balance of learning experiences for both parties. It seems however that this is a relatively unusual relationship, since most often it is the mentor who is giving in learning terms and not receiving. The mentor receives something quite different: the satisfaction of seeing someone develop and get appointed to more senior jobs.

Clutterbuck sets out the benefits and disadvantages of the mentoring situation. He also describes the phases in the mentor-protégé relationship and the problems which can arise from it, such as jealousy where the relationship is known and the problems of identifying an effective pairing. Benefits of mentoring in addition to direct coaching include bringing the protégé into contact with activities and thought processes at higher level in the organization and perhaps providing the learner with a better understanding of the structure of a company in terms of culture, rules of the game and internal politics.

One of the most important pieces of work has been that of Kram,[7] who identified the significance of phases in the mentor relationship through a detailed study with 'pairs'. Most particularly she identified the differences likely to arise when the relationship with the protégé is with a young adult as compared with a mid-life adult.

What then is the conclusion from this conflicting information about the frequency of mentor relationships? From my own observation of managerial relationships, my view is that mentoring is much less present than recent literature suggests. Even more importantly the literature deals in generalizations about the nature of the relationship and says little about the learning aspects. Specific comments about what people actually learned and how they learned it are remarkably few. Expressions of general interest and concern, and even some discussions from time to time between a mentor (prospective) and a protégé (unaware), have not yet been shown to be significant learning experiences.

Peers

The slightly more academic word 'peers' is used in preference to 'colleagues' to identify managers at precisely the same level; colleagues would embrace bosses and subordinates also. There were few references in our discussions to learning from peers. It is true we did not ask about it specifically, but in the process of describing how managers had learned peers did not figure. Perhaps once again an individual learns from mutual exchanges with colleagues without necessarily attaching the learning to the colleagues. He may attribute the experience to his own wisdom in understanding what came out of an exchange rather than allow his peer the distinction of removing the scales from his eyes (as compared with pulling the wool over them, as sometimes happens with peers).

One of the most fascinating insights we had into the ways in which peers worked together came from descriptions of relatively informal meetings at the top. In several cases organizations had decided to facilitate the processes of informal exchange by putting all directors together on one floor or in one building. As several of them described it to us, this enabled them to have easy exchanges with each other over problems and issues in a way which would not have been possible if they had been operating from buildings where they had separate empires.

These ad hoc and informal exchanges were sometimes complemented by regular weekly meetings to discuss the week's issues and problems. The meetings, which often had no agenda, no secretary and were not geared to decision taking, were intended to achieve more effective working both as individuals and as a group of directors. But the discussions with us brought out the fact that they were also learning experiences. 'Last week I was due to go and meet the ambassador of another country. I had never been involved either with that country or with an ambassador before. I took this into our weekly meeting and without asking directly for guidance on what to look out for, I actually received a lot of help from my colleagues.'

In another organization the comment was 'We have eliminated a lot of the walls that used to exist between us managerially by meeting together regularly. We know there are colleagues who have different experience from our own which we can call on. I have several times gone in with a problem on which I have developed an answer and really I thought I was just looking for communication and support. I came out with different and frankly better answers to the problems.'

Such experiences not only help to produce managerial answers but provide both the opportunity for and the actuality of learning on the part of those involved. They collect facts as one element of knowledge and learning, and they pick up ideas on different approaches to problems and different decision-making processes.

This is an area worthy of further investigation and discussion because many of the relationship issues, particularly those of power, between a boss and a subordinate do not exist to the same degree between peers. A learning relationship ought to be easier than with a boss/subordinate or even a mentoring relationship. One significant difference is that the relationship is much more mutual in that both participants are givers and receivers. Kram and Isabella[8] give an interesting summary of what would be possible in such a relationship, without however establishing how frequent such a relationship is in practice. In many ways this seems a more fruitful because less potentially stress-bound relationship from a learning point of view. It is possible to obtain information from peers, to discuss career strategies or get job-related feedback, or in the more adventurous relationships to get personal feedback, friendship and emotional support. However, even the innovative work of Kram and Isabella has identified broad relationship issues rather then discussing specific learning processes.

One additional finding from our survey was that although nearly all our directors worked on main boards which included non-executive directors, none of them mentioned a relationship with a non-executive director, and certainly none of them indicated that they had ever learned anything from these non-executive colleagues on the board. The absence of comment suggests that a potentially important source of learning from people exposed to different business situations and with different business experience is at present being missed by directors.

Subordinates

One or two directors mentioned specific experiences with subordinates where they saw themselves as being the learners rather than the subordinate. One director commented that from several subordinates in succession he learned that there was always more than one solution and particularly always more than his own solution to a problem. Another director gave a fascinating account of taking responsibility for a department in which he had no previous experience. Interesting the learning was not about the functional content: 'He was very good both at analysis and subsequent decision-taking. It was enriching for me. He saw things I did not see. Not only was this a good experience for me at the time, but it has stayed with me subsequently as something which I think I do better than I did before having this chap work for me.'

While many senior managers are prepared to accept that their progress up the organization depends on having good quality people underneath them, it is much more rare to find managers prepared to say that they learned from subordinates in this way. Perhaps there is a particular reluctance to do so because of the obvious status and power issues involved. However, it seems to be another area in which the learning process ought to be recognized as based solidly on real managerial activities rather than being an 'invented' learning relationship.

Networking

One of the characteristics of management is that managers achieve things by combinations of power, authority and influence. One of the most fascinating aspects of the work of John Kotter[9] was that managers quite frequently get things done not through direct apparent authority but through influence, which they exercise through networks. Networks consist of a vast range of people with whom the manager is in contact. In terms of line responsibility he may direct those working for him, but elsewhere the manager influences rather than directs.

This provides an additional collection of managers who are not bosses, may be peers and are not direct subordinates. They are however a store-house of ideas and information representing different kinds of interest and different experiences. They therefore provide potentially the information-based knowledge which is one part of learning, as well as a range of opportunities to see how other managers behave and a source of advice. Such managers can be less threatening because of their distance managerially from the manager who wishes to learn. It may sometimes be easier for a manager to make a casual enquiry of someone in his network but outside his line relationship.

> I was dealing with a problem in an area in which I had very little experience. However, I did not want to show my immediate colleagues that I was not sure what to do, and I certainly wanted to present a good answer to my new boss. I made an excuse to go and see a chap in another division ostensibly about something else. I knew he was pretty much an expert in the thing that was bothering me. I raised it incidentally and got some excellent ideas not only on the particular problem but on how I could approach similar issues in the future. I really learned from that guy; I don't know if he realized how little I knew, but he certainly helped me.

Requirements for learning from others

The process described in Chapter 2 as Type 2 Management Development applies equally to the processes described in this chapter. The learning that occurs accidentally and informally but not wholly satisfactorily which we described as Type 1 can be extended by greater awareness and some planned action into Type 2. In order to do so the manager must be aware of some of the processes which help or hinder such development.

Self-analysis

A more planned approach to learning from reality implies that the manager wishes to learn, as well as being capable of recognizing the opportunities shown in this chapter. That recognition comes from some kind of self-analysis on the needs for effective performance in the current job or in any future role. It also implies some level of awareness of aspects of the person as a 'whole self' as well as the person as 'managerial performer'. I describe this process as 'opening out' and ways of doing this are discussed in Chapter 12.

Self-development

The idea that managers will attempt to learn only those things which they have identified for themselves as learning needs, and that they will tend to learn best from the ways they choose for themselves, is reflected in the actual experience of the people we spoke to. The principles of self-development set out in Chapter 12 can be sustained through the kind of real work experiences described in this chapter and the previous one. It is precisely by centring development processes on the immediate world around, and insisting that the manager works harder at controlling his own destiny from a development point of view, that the core principle of development as a process 'done with' rather than 'done to' is best put into effect.

Trust

The process of sharing understanding, commitment, action as identified here is neither natural nor easy for managers (or indeed perhaps for anybody). Few of us are ready to reveal everything we might know about an individual. Lear's otherwise favourite daughter Cordelia was dismissed from his presence because she gave him what she perceived to be the unvarnished truth rather than using an element of tact.

Exchanges about learning opportunities, processes and achievements of the nature of those spelled out here need to be taken in small steps so that trust can be mutually developed, rather than in huge jumps or at the gallop. One of the essential differences in adult learning as compared with that of children is that adults think they have much more to lose by exposing themselves, whereas children are unaware that they actually have anything to lose. Perhaps as a consequence adults learn less because they risk less. Not all managers are good at identifying risks, or at taking them, in their normal managerial life, so they are unlikely to be better equipped to take risks as learners. Certainly they will not take risks if they are punished after the first risky sharing of concerns or requests for help. Trust is something which is necessary, not readily offered, and easily lost in the processes.

A learning group

The concept of a Learning Community has been developed in recent years. The idea is that a group can commit itself to learning goals as a group, and work together to achieve them, rather than simply operating as individuals with personal goals. The concept has largely been applied in structured development processes off the job. However, the idea that a group of managers could commit themselves to certain learning goals and apply this commitment in their normal managerial work has great potential. It is best to build on existing processes designed to encourage effective working relationships in a group. The attempt to build a learning community in a real managerial situation which has no other communal objective is likely to be a failure. If however it is built on a genuine dedication to working effectively as a group in pursuit of both organizational and team process objectives then the addition of a learning goal – the development of a review process on 'how are we doing as a learning group?' – could bring substantial benefit.

The learning processes

Stages of the learning process were shown in the model (Figure 3.1) at the beginning of Chapter 3, using familiar managerial words. The stages are best expressed as a learning cycle (Honey and Mumford, adapted from Kolb) (Figure 4.1).

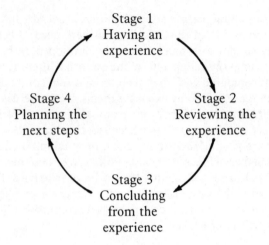

Figure 4.1 The learning cycle

Discussions with directors showed that they derived a great deal from the process described as having experience. They had also, sometimes consciously, more often unconsciously, developed a general view as a result of what they had learned from acting. They had drawn some conclusions from it. They had completed the learning sequence by carrying through what they believed they had learned either by tackling the same problem in a different way or by applying what was learnt to a different kind of problem.

Many of them, however, had been relatively weak or certainly least conscious at the stage of thinking about the results of the action phase. The processes very often lacked this reviewing or reflecting element, or had lacked it up to the point of the discussion with us.

Not only was this reflecting process often lacking along the way, but actually engaging in it through discussion with us often reminded or persuaded those with whom we were having the discussion that such an element was desirable and moreover attainable, even in the busy managerial life which they led. While, therefore, their descriptions of learning centred not only on managerial activity but on the action element rather than the thinking element, they were quite capable of recognizing in many cases that a reflective element could and should have been added. Full benefit from the kind of learning opportunities spelled out here will only be secured if

managers go through the learning cycle as often as possible in relation at least to the significant managerial events in which they are
involved. An example of this applied to a particular task discussion
was shown in Figure 2.3. Here it is appropriate to develop the argument a little further.

Not only did managers seem in general to have concentrated on
particular stages of the cycle. Their reaction to particular learning
activities varied from highly favourable to highly unfavourable.
These different reactions can be best explained by their different
preferences on how to learn. It is not true, as has been claimed, that
because all managers are 'doers' they always learn best from some
activity which provides 'doing'. Some managers actually prefer
learning experiences which provide a lot of opportunity to reflect.
Some managers like picking up the predigested solutions of others
and applying them where they see such an action as immediately
appropriate to a particular circumstance. The crucial significance
of understanding preferred learning processes and making the best
use of them is spelled out in Chapters 11 and 12.

Improving the learning process

The experience of directors given here is both encouraging and
alarming. Encouraging because there are good examples of learning
from a wide variety of experiences, discouraging because so many
of the opportunities are not recognized or not used to the full. The
inevitable and appropriate concentration on task performance has
been allowed to stunt the potential growth of learning experiences.
Yet this stunting process is unnecessary, because managers could
choose to manage the way they learn from others, balancing the
task and learning processes.

References

1   Mumford, A., 'The role of the boss in helping subordinates to
    learn' in B Taylor and G. Lippitt (ed.), *Management Development
    and Training Handbook*, 2nd edn., McGraw-Hill, London,
    1984
2   Gabarro, J. and Kotter, J., 'Managing your boss', *Harvard Busi-
    ness Review*, Jan.–Feb., 1980

3   Clutterbuck, D., *Everyone Needs a Mentor*, IPM 1985
4   Bennis, W. and Nanus, B., *Leaders*, Harper & Row, New York, 1985
5   Roche, G.R., 'Much ado about mentors', *Harvard Business Review*, Jan.–Feb., 1979
6   Pimlott, B., *Hugh Dalton*, Macmillan Paperback, London, 1986
7   Kram, K., 'Phases of the mentor relationship', *Academy of Management Journal*, vol. 6, no. 4, 1983
8   Kram, K., 'Alternatives to mentoring', *Academy of Management Journal*, vol. 8, no, 1, 1985
9   Kotter, J.P., *The General Managers*, Free Press, New York, 1982

5 Learning off the job

For most directors in our survey, the most frequent and most significant learning experiences had been centred on the job in the way indicated in the previous chapter. Some had also been influenced by processes of learning away from the job. Where this had occurred it was most often through a course, but we identified in addition some relevant learning experiences or processes which took place away from the job but were not part of a formal programme.

Courses differ from the processes we have described so far because they are explicitly aimed at learning. Whereas the processes of learning from and within jobs centre primarily on the task objective, courses are focused primarily on a learning objective. They may, as we shall see later, be designed to produce learning by the provision of tasks within the learning context. It is indeed precisely the attractiveness of undertaking tasks within a course which makes some training programmes acceptable and perhaps influential. However even in those programmes where task and learning are combined most fully, for example in Action Learning, the main objective is learning.

Courses therefore are likely to be perceived in a different way from the on-the-job processes described so far. As processes explicitly designed for learning, they might be more efficient than learning derived from normal task processes. They may on the contrary suffer from being removed from the normal work environment, which tends to encourage the view that the only way to learn is from real work.

It is very desirable that management development should be seen as a total process, in which different methods of learning are offered to individuals to meet their individual needs and the preferred processes of learning. The provision of such range of options was, we found, very much the exception even within those organizations which were relatively sophisticated in management development terms. The manager when undertaking managerial work in the normal managerial environment is on familiar and relatively understandable ground. The manager on a course is playing a different game on someone else's ground. Some of the comments which follow are explained not merely by the appropriateness or otherwise of the course content but by the extent to which managers are prepared to play by rules set by officials (trainers and educators) with different priorities and interests.

Why attend courses at all?

As I showed in an earlier book in more detail,[1] managers should attend a course when all the following criteria are met:

The course is designed to provide skills or knowledge, or to influence attitudes, in areas of significance to the organization.

The problems and oportunities which the manager will be better equipped to meet can most effectively be tackled through a formal training course.

The manager is committed to personal improvement and sees the course as a means to that end.

The organization as a whole, and the managers' superiors in particular, demonstrate through their priorities and action their belief in courses.

The course is provided at the right stage in the individual's development.

The course is properly resourced in terms of tutors and material.

Fellow participants on the programme represent an acceptable mix.

The methods of learning employed on the course are appropriate in content and acceptable to the individual.

While these criteria could be applied to any proposal that a manager should attend a course, there are other dimensions to the judgement, not least a clear view on whether the course is about skills or techniques, about knowledge or about attitudes. At the more senior levels particularly, it may be argued that a course is about none of these but about 'widening the intellectual horizon' of the managers involved. Others see a course as potentially concerned with self-understanding either through work on exercises and diagnostic instruments specifically designed to that end, or more generally through the encouragement of reflection during and at the end of a programme.

The general case for education and training can be based on the need to compete with other countries and a disbelief that management can possibly be undertaken without educational support. The heads of two of our leading management schools have expressed strong views.

Tom Kempner[2] criticizes the British anti-intellectual tradition which devalues education and training: 'This attitude is strong in business and many of its members not only believe in pragmatism – the cult of so called common sense and practical relevance – but its proponents are generally ill equipped to distinguish between fact and fancy. Their limited initial education and lack of subsequent training does not provide an adequate background for making judgements about the development of their successors. It is unwise to allow the people who got you into the mess to determine the training of the next generation.'

Professor Sir James Ball in his valedictory lecture[3] said: 'I believe that Britain's competitive position in the world relative to our leading competitors has been profoundly influenced by the typical British attitude of being unwilling to acknowledge the importance of intellectual ability in the conduct of practical affairs.' While accepting that most of the individual's development and learning takes place on the job he believed that management education has been a successful contributor. However, 'management education should also not be regarded as remedial treatment. It is for those whose relative performance would in any event have been better than those around them. In a significant sense the best people need and are capable of benefiting from education more than others.'

By implication, therefore, Professor Ball's argument would be particularly appropriate in relation to people on their way to the top, since in principle these clearly must be 'better than those around them'.

Kempner's case, however, is at least in part that the processes described in earlier chapters will be insufficient because of the quality of our existing management. His case is presumably that the prime influence of on-the-job development should be replaced by formal training. In Ball's case this proposition is extended only to a managerial meritocracy, with a clear recognition also of the significance of on-the-job development. A course may be the most effective way of developing skills precisely because Type 1 Management Development is so inefficient. Compare, for example, the incompetence of a manager who has not been trained to conduct selection interviews with someone who has attended a good course.

We did not distinguish in our survey between management education and training. There is no general agreement in either literature or practice as to the difference. Some people hold that education is what occurs in an external institution such as a college, business school or management centre, whereas training is what occurs in an organization's own training centre. Others believe that training is job-specific, whereas education deals with broader issues, but that either might be provided in any institution. Such disagreements confirmed our decision to concentrate on the content and objectives of courses.

'Own organization' courses

In our discussions with directors we asked them to talk about their experienced on internal and external courses. I have chosen here to distinguish between 'own organization' and 'open' courses. This is because some organizations mount courses entirely for their own people but run them outside the organization both physically and in terms of the preponderant contribution of tutors from a consultancy or business school.

We found that only a few organizations provide a full catalogue of management training courses. They offer a range of skills and usually also an ascending level in the status of those attending the courses, if not necessarily of difficulty in the course content. Rather more organizations provide a limited range of courses, and a few, normally the smaller ones, provide absolutely nothing internally.

The range of internal provision is larger than would have been available to the directors we saw when they were going through lower and middle management, though some of them had not taken advantage of the courses which were available. Only a small minority had been exposed to a substantial number of internal training courses. We found that where managers were supposed to attend a standard list of courses some of those at the top had not done so and the organizations themselves seemed unaware of this. The total quantity of training experienced was therefore smaller than organizations often presumed.

More important was the quality of experience as perceived by the directors. The view they expressed could be seen to have affected not only their own appetite for further training but also that of colleagues.

There were a number of comments about the significance and influence of courses. 'The course was intended to help change the cultural climate. It was not designed to teach us anything in the conventional sense but to help us understand what we wanted to do and to point us in an agreed direction.' Another director described a course which had looked specifically at strategic management issues in relation to the company's own processes. She perceived it as highly effective because it combined a high level of professional competence with a very obvious business need. It filled a gap in the experience of the managers attending the programme. In addition to its contribution to her own personal development, it added to her firm conviction that management development must be tied to specific business needs if it was to be effective.

My then managing director thought that the board and the top team did not know what a strategy was let alone work to a common one. He insisted that we all went on a one week strategic management course tailored for our company by an outside specialist. It was fantastic, it gave me a totally different perspective on what I was doing, indeed on the whole of my business life. I would never have thought of doing anything like that at the level I was at in the company if the managing director had not insisted.

These examples were drawn from a stage of development closest to that of appointment to the main board. It is perhaps not surprising that they figured more largely in the recollection of these managers than anything they had attended previously.

There were two cases where board members had taken a course originally designed for managers below board level. In neither case had the argument for doing so been presented baldly as helping the directors to improve their own skills. The argument had been that the effectiveness of the programme at lower levels would be greater if directors knew what it was about. Directors also quoted earlier experiences particularly concerned with basic managerial techniques such as chairing meetings or interviewing which they thought had played a helpful part in their development. There were also a few critical references to internal courses regarded as a waste of time with no useful product.

Most comments were between these two extremes. Directors often struggled to remember courses they had attended, and when they did remember tended to make neutral comments about them. We always tried to encourage our directors to talk about what they had done as a consequence of a course, since for most courses one objective is that managers should do something additional or different. The majority of comments, to which we gave the description 'grey', did not reveal much direct application from the course. The 'grey' comments tended to be such as 'I remember feeling that what we covered was interesting, but if there was anything of specific application in my job afterwards I cannot remember any particular relationship'.

It might be argued that some courses are not designed to provide techniques or skills which are directly applied. The effectiveness of courses in meeting different objectives could not be assessed through this survey. What we were able to assess was the extent to which whatever had been provided, against whatever course objectives, had been seen by directors as a major contribution to their development. The answer was that the influence was relatively small in comparison with other experiences. It may be that for some directors significant internal courses did not exist when they were going through junior and middle management. It may be that the quality and effectiveness of such programmes was much lower some years ago. Moreover the internal training courses of many organizations stop two or three levels below the main board, so that such courses may have been taken many years ago. It may also be that recollection dims over a prolonged period of time. On the other hand directors who could not remember anything significant about some internal courses they had attended could often identify something else of significance in their development many years back. Since directors were being asked to focus on experiences explicitly about learning, the fact that they gave such relatively low marks to them suggests that courses may indeed not have been very powerful learning experiences.

The explanation probably lies in the failure of managers to identify needs and a consequent lack of commitment, and in the ineffectiveness of the learning processes adopted. Particularly at the more senior levels, there should also be a results-oriented approach to business problems and opportunities, using the course to work on real problems rather than acquiring knowledge and skills which are then supposed to be applied outside the course. Examples of the application of such an approach in the United States are given by Bolt[4]. Since some of the concepts apply equally to 'own organization' and 'open' courses, the process is reviewed more fully after the next section, in which we review open courses.

Several directors commented to us that they had learned not as course attenders but as performers, particularly on internal courses:

I had to prepare for a 90-minute session on our senior internal management course. It was the first time for several years that I was forced to look at what I was doing personally and what my division was doing. I drew up a framework and prepared some models. Not only did it raise some questions in my mind about some of our priorities, but the process of thinking through some of our relationships really drew together the learning I had absorbed unconsciously about why things were like that.

Another case illustrated a rather different kind of learning process:

Like a lot of Chief Executives I go along and participate in courses. I pick up a lot from talking to people informally over meals and in the bar and I would not discount that as a useful part of learning. The really significant thing for me however is being exposed to sharp questioning by my own people on a course. I learn a lot from the things they're interested in, and even more from the questions they ask and even more from the comments and suggestions they make. We employ very bright people and I can pick up a great deal from their suggestions on how we can improve the running of the business.

Finally a comment again different in kind:

I share a session on our senior management course with a lecturer from a business school. Listening to him answer questions from the course participants is a splendid way of my learning the things that they are learning also. I have never been on a management course myself, and at least this one session is a partial replacement for that.

'Open' courses

Even fewer directors had attended an 'open' course than had attended an 'own organization' programme. We met five MBAs and 12 managers who had attended a significant post-experience course. Our definition for the latter was a programme of four weeks or more, a definition we developed from our own experience with managers and with course providers, both of whom see a divide at around four weeks. Only one director had been exposed to both an MBA and another post-experience programme, and only one director had attended two management courses of four weeks or more.

The quantitative impact of open programmes is therefore even less than that of 'own organization' courses. The qualitative picture was very similar in that a small number of directors were profoundly affected by an open course but there were many 'grey' comments. While there were practically no examples of directors condemning an 'own organization' course, there were several in relation to an open course.

I went on a four-week management programme which was one of the most frustrating experiences of my life. I am never going near a management course again, and I am very unwilling that any of

my people should. All the examples were drawn from manufacturing and retail operations, with no reference at all to the kind
of service world in which I work, let alone the financial part of
that world. I could not relate what they were describing to the
business that I run.

I went on a course at a major business school which was supposed to be the distinguishing mark that I was going to make it to
the main board. It did absolutely nothing for me in the job which
I was doing then, and I have found none of it useful since I got on
to the main board. The most interesting learning experience was
actually being part of a group which went and complained to the
faculty about the programme. Most of the faculty did their standard turns with no reference to the composition of our particular
group, and clearly none of them had ever actually tried to implement in business the things which they were describing to us.

Course experiences which had greater relevance to the directors'
current activities evoked more favourable comments. About a
leadership programme actually taken when a main board member:
'In some ways it was a summarizing or concluding experience. It
confirmed what I had begun to recognize, as I gradually changed
from being entirely interested in my own individual achievement to
team achievement.'

It is often asserted that MBA programmes equip managers to
operate at main board level rather than at managerial level. The
following comment was the most specific of those we received: 'I
could not do my job effectively now without having acquired these
basics. I can deal with specialist functions in which I have no direct
job experience. It also taught me that there is a sequence in
tackling problems.'

One woman director commented about a long management
course:

It formalized a lot of things for me. Many of them I was doing
already, but more because they seem sensible than because of
any formal discipline. It did two other things. It gave me a good
grounding in accounting which I hate. It also got me used to
striving. I was the only woman on the course and one of the
oldest. The competition tuned up the learning curve. I suddenly

realized that my brain was working in over drive and that I loved working that way. I have been in that gear ever since.

Again it was only a minority of those directors who had attended open courses who rated them as very significant in their personal development. The extended length of open courses had not necessarily produced any greater impact. Directors referred to short courses from which they had picked up techniques over one or two days.

Given again that they were attending an experience specifically designed for learning, which often lasted between 6 and 10 weeks, the fact that some directors could identify no precise benefits seems alarming. It is less surprising for anyone experienced in this field because it has been a sadly recurrent finding over many years.

Some course providers would respond that they are not aiming to provide identifiable benefits in the sense of immediately applicable techniques or skills. A more sophisticated excuse is that the learning process was so brilliantly designed in relation to the real managerial needs of those attending that the learning was incorporated in normal managerial practice without the conscious recognition of the manager. But it seems more likely, as with 'own organization' courses, that directors indeed learned very little that was of practical use. 'Open' programmes are provided by a wide range of people and institutions: by middle-level consultants perhaps operating as one-man bands, and by high-level gurus paid expensively first for name and then for quality. They are provided by a range of training and management consultancies, and by management education centres and business schools. There are significant differences of price and quality with no necessary correlation between the two.

A great deal of public debate revolves on how much management education ought to be provided, of what length, and whether an academic qualification for management is desirable. It is necessary to look briefly at some of those issues. If lengthy formal management education processes are desirable for managers, it would be perverse to argue that the people at the top of organzations do not need them. Indeed those a the top ought to be the best trained and educated managers.

An MBA for the top?

We interviewed five MBAs. There are perhaps between 8000 and 10 000 working in the UK. Japan also produces very few. The USA currently produces between 65 000 and 70 000 MBAs a year, and Harvard alone has produced 32 000.

The concept of intensive study to become fully equipped as a professional manager has not taken root in the UK. One reason may be that as Professor Kempner seems to suggest, British managers are profoundly anti-intellectual. The managers themselves point to the supposed lack of practical relevance of the MBA course. Perhaps even more powerful are similar criticisms arising from within US business schools themselves, first from Livingston[6] and more recently from Leavitt[7] and Behman and Levin.[8] Particular criticisms are that most MBA programmes concentrate too much on conceptual processes of analysis, that there is too little integration of functional subjects and that they are over-concerned with issues of high-level policy and strategy which most students will be unable to influence.

It might be thought that the MBA would be especially appropriate for developing directors precisely because of a concentration on concepts and strategy. Our survey encountered some who had found it to be so. A British report by Forrester[9] presents an optimistic view of the success and future of MBA programmes. Since 48 per cent of the MBAs interviewed said that the contents were either 'of no use' or 'of peripheral use', the grounds for optimism seem rather shaky.

The discussion centres on the concept of relevance. My own institution's MBA is based on the view that, for manager and director alike, conceptual and strategic knowledge must be accompanied by the ability to take action in real situations and to learn from doing so. Traditional business school programmes seem not to have taken account of the analyses of actual management processes offered by Rosemary Stewart, John Kotter and Henry Mintzberg (see Chapter 8). They employ teaching processes valued by the educator rather than learning processes open to the manager. Nor have they been very responsive to the idea that what they teach, and how they teach, may not fit managerial needs. The general response of business schools to criticism has been much like that of the Englishman abroad who, faced with foreigners unable to speak English, speaks louder.

If there are problems about flagship management education courses, why do managers continue to attend them, and what can we expect them to do well in developing people for the top? The better courses certainly should help with the following:

changes in the social and technical environment

changes in markets

information about management processes and the basis for choice between them

checking the culture and beliefs in the manager's own organization

examining and perhaps changing the assessment of the manager's own past experience

systems for integrating the professional functions within management, eg marketing and finance

comparing self with others

This list emphasizes those aspects of management which are particularly relevant at top levels, as compared with managment skills which the manager has already acquired lower down, or detailed knowledge of a functional operation.

When describing benefits from these external programmes, our directors often indicated particularly the benefits they had secured from the processes of exchange between themselves. Comparison of themselves with others was on the whole believed to be a warming and satisfying exierince. 'I thought managers from big name companies were bound to be much better than I was; I found something different. They were not necessarily brighter or more skilled than me, but they did have sometimes interestingly different experience. The course gave me a lot more confidence about myself.'

Some might argue that this was a strange result from a process which was generally presumed to be about challenge rather than complacency. Yet, managers seemingly learn a tremendous amount from each other, often in the informal exchanges at least as much as in the structured small group gatherings, and often a great deal more than they learn in formal main group sessions. They have been saying this for years, yet most educational programmes are designed on the assumption that the real learning occurs in the formal sessions to which most time is allotted.

If the providers of education and training had been listening properly over the years they might have realized that there is some dissatisfaction with what is occurring in the formal sessions; and that managers talk informally about precisely those real problems, real situations and differences of experience that most formal sessions ignore. The powerful exchanges of personal anecdotes are registered as significant learning experiences whereas the structured content and managerial theories in the formal programme are not.

Managerial work away from the job

Several directors commented on what they learned from visiting other companies and talking to other executives. In some cases they had spend time talking with important figures in industry or commerce. Jobs involving a lot of contact with customers lent themselves particularly to this kind of process. Rather similar opportunities existed for people working in the financial services area, which tended to involve visits to companies which in turn involved reviewing the way in which they had achieved their success. As with learning on the job, learning from these visits tended to be something recognized subsequently through our discussion rather than having been designed and managed as a learning experience at the time.

One of our directors mentioned that his continued learning processes were enhanced by his practice of returning to a business school at which he had attended a programme. He went back once or twice a year to discuss issues with one or two members of the faculty. He regarded this as a process which both kept him up to date and challenged his mental processes on issues of concern to him.

Another director had learned through participation in a Commonwealth Study Conference concerned with the impact of industry on the community and vice versa. This involved a group of managers, trade unionists and public servants in a study tour.

The experience really had a tremendous impact on me because we looked at very real issues from our different perspectives and learned an enormous amount from what we saw and from each other. Not only did I learn a lot during the three weeks which stayed with me, I am still learning from it. I retain contact with people from the tour. It had the greatest single impact upon me of any learning experience I have had.

Another learning process connected with a formal training experience was that of a director who regularly attended reunion dinners from a course he had attended some years before. Discussion of issues with people outside his own organization, but with whom he had shared a significant experience, was a process he found extremely helpful. The formal meetings were with a fairly large group of people, but in addition he had retained contact with one or two individuals with whom he might have separate meetings during the year. This was rather similar to the process described in the previous chapter of working with peers within the organization.

While all of these examples have a clear connection with the job of a director, we encountered one other example of a non-managerial kind involving the director's experience as a magistrate. 'You have to listen, sift evidence, weigh options and make decisions. Then you have to influence other people. When you become Chairman as I did as well, you have to chair other people who are often very articulate and sometimes challenging you.' He saw this as adding to the experience which he gained within his own organization.

Awareness of this kind however was very unusual amongst the people we saw. Although they were often involved in committees, industry associations and charities outside the business, the activity was nearly always seen purely in terms of its overt objective, and as with on-the-job learning but even more strongly there was little recognition of the opportunity to learn from the activity. While this is a missed chance from a development point of view it is very understandable, because the activities themselves are probably seen as relatively marginal. One director had been very much involved in Industry Year in 1986, but he had seen it entirely as a process of putting something back into the community and representing his own organization. If there were opportunities to learn from the people with whom he was associated, he had not perceived them.

Learning at home

Many managers spend time at home working on office papers; however they are not doing different work but merely the same work in a different place. None of them suggested that they used this time in a way wholly different from the way they used the time at the office – for example to engage in more reflective or planning processes. Chapter 2 quoted a manager who sent time at home thinking about his successes during the day, but he actually used the same kind of thinking processes when travelling in a train or car, in breaks in the office and in other gaps in the day.

It would be an interesting area for future research to see whether managers do different things in a different kind of way at home compared with their normal work processes. Experience outside the survey suggests that some managers use the home experience to discuss work problems with their spouses. A few of our participants certainly mentioned the participation of their wives in discussions about career choice. (In our small sample of women directors discussion with their husbands was not mentioned, but this may have been accidental.)

There are a variety of other processes for learning at home, which I have spelled out in detail.[10] The opportunity to observe and learn from the activities in which we and our friends are engaged at home, to monitor reactions to particular kinds of behaviour, is one which rarely seems to be taken up. Again the reason probably is that such activities are seen as distant from the reality of work, and indeed there is a justifiable argument for saying that managers want to relax at home and not set themselves learning targets. It seems likely that managers often behave rather differently at home compared with the office, and if such behaviour were to be seen as a deliberate change than its adoption and the effect of it would be a learning experience.

The most obvious process of learning would be that of reading. In Chapter 3 we looked at the possibility of learning from the literary efforts of people who are themselves managers. If in this chapter we stretch the coverage to the vast range of books and articles pro-

duced by people who are not managers, the number of readers will
still be low. At the time of our survey the two most popular books
were Iacocca's (mentioned in Chapter 3) and *In Search of
Excellence*.[11] A minority of managers read articles in *Management
Today* or the *Harvard Business Review*, usually when sent to them by
a colleague. While the relatively low addiction to reading was confirmation of what is already known, we found that for the minority
who did read the learning opportunities involved were unnecessarily restricted. While reading is by definition a solitary event, the
learning process involved does not have to be purely solitary. In
Chapter 13 I show how these solitary reading processes could be
converted into more effective learning experiences, for example
through discussion with colleagues.

References

1   Mumford, A., *Making Experience pay*, McGraw-Hill, Lon-
    don, 1980
2   Kempner, T., 'Education for management in five countries',
    Journal of General Management, vol. 9, no. 2, 1983–84
3   Ball, R.J., 'Management education in the UK', Stockton Lec-
    ture, London Business School, Feb., 1983
4   Bolt, J.F.,'Tailor executive development to strategy', *Harvard
    Business Review*, Nov./Dec. 1985, pp. 168–76
5   Hunt, J., 'The Case for Harvard', *Chief Executive*, Jan.
    1985
6   Livingston, J.S., 'Myth of the well educated manager', *Har-
    vard Business Review*, Jan.–Feb. 1971, pp. 79–89
7   Leavitt, H., 'What is right and what's wrong', *London Business
    School Journal*, vol. no. 1, Summer, 1983
8   Behrman, J.N. and Levin, R.I., 'Are business schools doing
    their job?', *Harvard Business Review*, Jan.–Feb., 1984, pp. 140–
    47
9   Forrester, J., 'A study of the practical uses of the MBA', BIM,
    London, 1984
10 Mumford, A., 'Managers developing learning abilities at

home', *Programmed Learning and Educational Technology*, vol. 22, no. 4, 1985, pp. 362–67

11   Peters, T. and Waterman, R., *In Search of Excellence*, Harper & Row, New York, 1983

6 Learning from courses

One of the common features of our discussions, supported by our own experience and a wide range of literature, is a lack of conviction about the effectiveness of learning from courses. One explanation has been touched on in the previous chapter. Trainers and educators have different concepts from most managers of the management process and the learning process in which they are engaged.

It is not simply that lazy managers are unwilling to consider those propositions about management that educators want to discuss, or that managers want practical processes and illustrations to the total exclusion of stimulating theory. Nor perhaps surprisingly do trainers and educators share a common position of being intellectuals crying in the wilderness. Not only are many trainers a long way from being intellectuals or indeed even particularly thoughtful about the processes in which they are involved. A good many business school academics seem to be equally uninterested in the process in which they are engaged, namely that of helping managers to learn.

In addition many of them are knowledgeable about their subject but wholly lack the capacity of the real intellectual to integrate their own knowledge with that of other specialists. Observe a knowledgeable marketing professor wriggling with impatience as managers spoil his marketing case study by diverting it into a discussion about the interpersonal relationships involved.

It is however true that on the whole both trainers and educators emphasize analysis, together with the ability to justify a conclusion drawn from that analysis and to deliver that justification either orally or in writing in persuasive and intelligible form. Their values and their processes cause them to design programmes which emphasize these abilities. Managers value much less the processes by which a decision is made and implemented. They operate in a managerial world in which they do not have the luxury of hours of analysis and thought and must seize opportunities rather that operate to some grand design.

The difference is illustrated by a well-known cricketing story. The great Yorkshire slow left-arm bowler Wilfred Rhodes was bowling to a young batsman at the nets and trying to get him to put his feet in the right position. The young batsman constantly hit Rhodes into the vast open spaces. 'Look where your feet are', said Rhodes. 'Look where the bloody ball is', said the young batsman who was hitting sixes so effectively; his coach was interested in something else. Educators and trainers have simply ignored the reality of how top managers work. They are not to be condemned for having no personal experience of this and there are equivalent cases of managers who are quite incapable of describing their experiences in a way which is useful to others. The criticism of educators and trainers is that lacking the experience themselves they have ignored the work of those who have revolutionized our thinking about the processes of management, the great trinity of Steward, Mintzberg and Kotter as described in Chapter 8.

Nor is managerial reality met by simply getting managers to 'do things' on courses. Management trainers particularly have been extraordinarily active in producing simulations of real work – business games, interactive computer exercises, role plays, case studies, task centred projects within courses. The most powerful way to learn however is not working on brilliantly contrived simulations but dealing with real management problems. Of course managers on the whole enjoy discussions more than even brilliantly delivered lectures. Many of them will certainly enjoy and perhaps even occasionally learn from business games, or outdoor management training in which the quality of learning sometimes seems to be equated with the discomfort involved in the exercise. But effective education and training processes are based on reality and use live management work as the core of the learning process.

If a company needs to produce a business strategy, a one-week course run by a stimulating and experienced guru can be a marvellous experience for at least some of the participants. Yet the process can be made more meaningful for many, and more valuable for all, if the concept of reality is employed. One company we worked with wanted a group of managers to produce certain strategies and plans by particular dates. We designed with them a programme which not only provided the appropriate tools in terms of knowledge and techniques but actually required them to work on the plans as an inherent part of the programme. The article already referred to by Bolt shows a similar kind of development in four organizations in the United States.

The essential principle involved is that of Action Learning, developed by Professor Reg Revans, the only major innovator in management education produced in the UK until the 1980s. Action Learning combines the process of undertaking work with learning about the process of managing. Normally it means working on a defined project and particularly working with colleagues in a group known technically as a 'set'. Action Learning evolved from dissatisfaction with traditional processes of conveying knowledge to managers who are often unwilling to receive it and not in a position to apply it anyway. It is based on the fundamentally simple but profound perception that managers can actually learn from the work they do, and learn particularly well by discussion with one another.

Once this great link has been established both conceptually and in practice, a third element, the learning process itself, becomes even more evident. This is discussed later in the chapter, and at greater length in Chapters 11 and 12. The fundamental association necessary for the effective design of courses is therefore:

> determination to deal with the reality of management as it applies to managers on the course, rather than give theoretical explanations of what management ought to be about

> use within the course of real management problems and opportunities, with real consequences derived from actual management accountabilities, rather that simulations of management problems

> learning methods appropriate to what the course aims to deliver, modified by the actual learning processes preferred by the participants on the course.

Implementation after a course

Courses designed according to these principles would significantly reduce the problems of transfer or re-entry frequently described in relation to traditional courses. The chances of managers learning things on a course which they cannot apply when they return are much reduced if they actually work on real problems as part of the programme.

Not all the re-entry problems are of course eliminated. Managers who go on high quality programmes may still be perceived as a threat to colleagues, to bosses and to the organizational culture at large. Nor should all training and education centres attempt to transform themselves into Action Learning institutions.

All courses ought to teach managers how to implement what they have learned. One or two business schools already do this by providing several days at the end of an extended programme when participants work on carrying through the things they have learned. One of the barriers here is that course designers characteristically squeeze in more content rather than spending time in implementation, which takes us back to the values of the course designers again.

I have run a series of workshops within one organization which was not centred on the managers undertaking a project or working in sets. They dealt with the reality of management problems arising from a changed organization structure and a desired change in management style. We did not simply face them with interesting knowledge about the differences between working in a matrix structure and their previous traditional organization structure. We caused them to work on these problems as redefined by their own experience in the organization, and to commit themselves to action within the workshop. On a different course, we provided nearly the whole of the last day of a five-day programme for managers from a variety of organizations to draw up their plans for action on their return. They presented and counselled each other on those plans.

Timing

I have already suggested that one of the problems with MBA programmes is that for many participants the timing is wrong; the content is appropriate for a still remote main board level. One of the reasons why directors felt that some experiences had been valuable was that not only had they related to issues of real concern but they had done so at the right time. This can occur even with relatively traditional programmes.

One manager was to change from managing one company to managing a group of companies, a shift characteristic of the move to main board level. The executive resource plan had identified the retirement date of the man he was to replace, and had identified him as the appropriate successor. The man in possession actually delayed his retirement by several months in order to allow his successor to attend a management programme. Not only would it have been more difficult for him to be released for an extended period once he had taken up the job, but it was obviously important that he should be trained in advance of the appointment.

Other points about courses

Internal and external programmes are rarely direct alternatives to each other. There may be priorities for individuals but there are usually significant differences which make an informed choice possible. These differences are shown in Figure 6.1

The most obvious point for top level managers, whether on or immediately below the board, is that external courses are very often geared as much to individuality and status as to content. If we want top managers to learn we must make it easy for them to do so, and it may not be easy if they are placed within an internal group. Specific suggestions on this matter and indeed others concerned with the personal development of existing main board directors are given in Chapter 13.

Attendance on either internal or external courses ought to be determined by a careful analysis of needs, as described in Chapters 11 and 12; indications of how such analysis can be undertaken even at top level are given in Chapter 13. It can scarcely be over-emphasized that failure to make such analysis of needs, and to secure a manager's acknowledgement of them, is one of the more obvious causes of dissatisfaction in people who attend courses which they think to be irrelevant. It is of no value that the course might help them to remedy a weakness which they do not recognize they have. Several of our directors had been sent on programmes with no prior discussion about what they would do for them and why they were being sent. Discussions with the personnel directors or their chief executives sometimes showed that the reasons were legitimate and benevolent, but if the manager himself has not been involved his attitude to the course is unlikely to be positive.

Own Organization	*Open*
Potentially specific to organization needs	Likely to be general
Can make use of company specific material	Use material from a variety of sources
Contained within organizational culture	May develop alternative views about organization culture
Probably focuses on company issues	Operates more widely in a general context
Participants more likely to feel they are being assessed	Participants more likely to feel they are not being assessed
Experience on offer is relatively narrow	Experience available from managers and faculty likely to be wider
Economic for groups of manager	Suitable for 'single' managers
Tutors may be perceived as 'junior'	Higher quality and/ or credibility of tutors

Figure 6.1 Comparison of 'own organization' and open programmes

The learning process has been mentioned in this chapter and will be discussed fully in Chapters 11 and 12. Since the book is about learning there is no need to apologize for its frequent appearance. It is a sad commentary on many other books about management development that while they discuss management development processes and methods in great detail the learning process is never discussed. Even worse, business schools and management training centres seem largely to ignore the process which is most central to their existence.

I used to think it merely paradoxical that institutions whose self-proclaimed purpose was to help managers to learn had no theory of learning which they used in the design of their programmes, nor did they ever discuss the learning process with participants. I now see it as a disastrous failure, and a cause in itself of the ineffectiveness of many programmes for individual managers. To find for example that on a two-year MBA programme the learning process is never discussed, and there is no attempt to help managers understand and sharpen their learning skills, is to recognize just how inappropriate the design of such a programme is. Since such activities are not undertaken on lengthy programmes it is less surprising that they are also missing from shorter ones. Ways in which this failure can be remedied are discussed in my monograph.[1]

Both in the UK and the United States the centres of management education have been centres for management teaching not management learning. One of the most illuminating comments by Professor Sir James Ball in the lecture quoted in the previous chapter is that he felt they were a 'long way from fulfilling a commitment in any formal sense to enable people to handle their own learning. They may do so, but we are not in my view in explicit control of that process.' I do not think that management teachers ought to be in control of the process, but I am absolutely sure that they ought to be contributing to it in a way which Professor Ball clearly indicates they have not done so far. One of the main purposes of any training and education process lasting more than one or two days should be to assist the manager to continue to learn after the experience. To treat courses as occasional interventions in management development is bad enough. To fail to connect managers to the reality of management is worse. To compound those errors by failing to teach managers the learning process is unforgivable.

Reference

1   Mumford, A., 'Learning to learn for managers', *Journal of European Industrial Training*, vol. 10, no. 2, 1986

7 Managing management development

The term 'management development' is said by Mant[1] to have existed in the United Kingdom only since 1951. While a few commercial and industrial organizations will have been carrying out some of the processes identified below for longer than that, organized management development in most of the organizations we visited was of much shorter life. Even some of the largest organizations had been taking a structured view of management development for only around five years.

The purpose of a management development scheme is to ensure that executives are developed or recruited and trained in sufficient numbers to sufficient standards to meet the specialist and general management requirements of a group in the short and the long term. Some organizations set an objective that all top management appointments should be filled from within, from people developed by the organization itself. Others set target figures for recruitment from outside or fill senior functional jobs from outside (eg finance or personnel).

The development of managers includes performance appraisal, the identification of individual training and development needs, the planning and review processes applying to these individual assessments and perhaps to the decision-making powers of those involved in making job movement or development decisions.

Appraisal procedures should be identified, and perhaps some guidance given in written form, possibly supplemented by training on carrying out the review and development task. The range of development processes which might be considered may be indicated either on an appraisal form or in some guidance booklet.

We did not encounter any organization which has a separate process for identifying the development of people for the main board. Whatever processes are applied to managers in general could be applied with extra energy and direction to top level managers.

We encountered some organizations of all sizes which made no attempt to plan the processes of management development to take people to the top. Some had no planned development at all, and in very large organizations the processes of decentralization and delegation of authority sometimes meant that planned processes might occur in some areas and not in others, with no intervention to ensure that people of appropriate quality were available for board appointments. In such organizations there is a conflict between the general management style of delegation and the particular need for the development of top managers. Some otherwise highly decentralized organizations decided to make some kind of intervention, taking the view that planning the financial and physical resources of the business might be rendered nugatory if the people at the top lacked the ability to manage these resources effectively.

The processes of planning

Three different methods of planning the top management resource were used:

> *Replacement Plans*, which essentially showed the jobs at the top level, who currently filled them, and who might replace them at retirement date or after some other change.

> *Succession Plans*, which in addition to covering replacements would identify the steps necessary to equip people for them. Plans might include such statements as 'Should be moved to get experience in another part of the business' and 'Should attend Harvard AMP next year'.

> *Resource Plans*, which would review not only the future succession but also current effectiveness.

It was clear that some organizations had only Replacement Plans although they described them as Succession Plans

Most frequently these plans, often drawn up through the Personnel Department, were discussed in relation to main board appointments through an executive committee of the main board or perhaps the main board itself. Usually this occurred on a single review day or half-day in the year, but sometimes the event was given greater significance by being held off site. The normal form of discussion would be that plans, charts and perhaps biographical or performance statements would be produced and put into a pack for the day. The content of such discussions characteristically centred on the kind of demonstration already given, namely job movements and courses. Those processes of development identified earlier as being most frequent and most central in the actual development of managers seem not to be discussed.

Several organizations were able to describe the specific benefits they had derived from such planning processes. One organization had reviewed its resources and decided that it had insufficient management potential for the longer term. It recruited middle managers, including two MBAs, with a ten-year time horizon. Fifteen years later their current board largely consisted of these managers.

The way in which an organization approaches management development may change over years, not only in moving from a wholly informal and unstructured approach to a more planned one, but by changes within a formal system. Organizations adopt a more structured process when they believe that they will not otherwise meet their objectives. It is only when they feel hurt by the absence of managers capable of operating at the top level that they begin to undertake processes designed to provide them. Management development is then an explicit response to business needs. The company mentioned in the previous paragraph is an example.

There can however be changes even in organizations which have previously undertaken planned management development. Perhaps the ownership has changed from private to public, with a recognition that running a public company requires different skills. Changes in structure also affect at least the content of formal management development. As one director said, 'Management development must go hand in hand with setting up profit centres if managers and ourselves are to learn and understand what is expected of us. I see management development as a powerful agent of change which must, by definition, be in step with business development.'

Changes in the nature of the business may also influence management development. Diversification may entail, especially for main board directors, the development of new skills and understanding.

It was interesting to note historical changes in the perspectives and priorities in management development. The earliest processes were very obviously geared to the development of 'crown princes'. These processes were then quite properly attacked as being too exclusive, and the development of managers as a total group became the norm for organizations interested in management development. There has been a reversion more recently to a different form of 'crown prince', since some organizations recognize that within the context of general management development there is a need to identify and make special provision for those who may make it to the top. Such organizations encountered substantial difficulties in actually identifying the people who were going to be the winners!

From the organization's point of view the purpose of planned development is to satisfy its own needs. We encountered very few organizations which referred to the development of the individual as being a goal in itself.

Profit centre and overseas experience

It is generally thought desirable that managers should have a range of functional experience before reaching the top (as discussed in Chapter 2). Formal schemes try to introduce both the concept and the reality of such experience. In many organizations it is also accepted that experience overseas and in running a profit centre is highly desirable. In the past the two were often combined, since multinationals who had companies abroad would provide both kinds of experience. As however such companies have moved increasingly towards providing local managers these opportunities have diminished. It may be that many managers in the future will reach the top with only lower level experience of working overseas. Although profit centre experience might be provided in the home country, the general belief was that even where subsidiary companies existed they were often less autonomous in practice than the overseas companies.

Job rotation

The planning of careers in the sense of planned job moves – job rotation – was frequently identified by organizations as the prime achievement of their management development schemes. Though few cases were quoted where an individual was put into a job largely for development reasons, they were well remembered: 'I was sent to do a job in an area which I had never been involved in before and about which I knew absolutely nothing. When I protested to my boss that I knew nothing about the job he smiled slightly, told me that was exactly the point, and told me to go away and think about why I was being put into it. It turned out to be a very important experience for me.'

Yet the preponderant factor in making appointments to a job was that the prospective job holder would do the job well. Not surprisingly most organizations and most managers on the way up saw the job content and the possibilities within the job as crucial. Development benefits were often very secondary and, most important from a development perspective, rarely discussed with the individual. Moves sometimes involved more than one individual in a chess-board approach with a number of pieces moved as part of a total strategy. Such moves were most frequently identified with particular job requirements and very seldom with development opportunity.

The paradox is that while a management development system will be trying to identify job opportunities as development opportunities, the management system itself is operating on different priorities. The system may be in a state of flux; changes in the business environment, in objectives, in organization structure and perhaps most importantly in the power of particular individuals influence the potential for planned job moves but perhaps reduce the actual number.

Organizations tended to claim a greater degree of planning and successful implementation than was recognized by the directors who were supposed to have been involved. If a scheme had existed during their career most of them thought it not to have been influential on their job moves. Decisions about which job they should go into were ascribed to the strength of feeling of the individual himself, to the particularly powerful influence of some figure in the organization, or to crises, luck or other factors. Sometimes directors themselves felt uncomfortable with this description of the reality they thought they had experienced. They would offer mild correctives suggesting that perhaps someone somewhere had been doing some planning.

At the very least therefore the system seems to have failed to communicate its operation to those involved. Organizations themselves explained that it was risky and difficult to communicate plans for job movements because a discussion of possibilities seemed to get translated into promises in the mind of the recipient. Part of the gap between their supposed plans and the statements of their directors was thus inevitable. It was also felt that directors might want to play down what they had experienced in terms of planned development if they had attributed their job movement entirely to their own exceptionally successful personal performance. Generally however directors attributed their movements, above a reasonable level of competence, to factors such as luck or changes in structure. It seems more reasonable therefore to accept that planning was less effective than organizations proclaimed.

The defensive explanations of personnel directors are understandable. But the likelihood of a manager being effectively developed for a job which has not been discussed, through job moves which in turn have not been discussed in terms of development processes, is much less than if the issues were actually discussed.

Identifying needs

The process of development through courses was discussed in the two previous chapters. In this chapter we need emphasize only that managers still seem to arrive on courses as the result of a process which is all too often chaotic and irresponsible. This is partly a consequence of elements of the formal system not working together. It may be that appraisal is supposed also to identify development needs, but that anything which emerges from this route is ignored by decision-making processes about courses. Powerful people in the organization, sometimes including personnel directors, experience themselves or hear about 'good' courses and then look around for other people to send on them. With this sort of failure in the process of identification preceding the arrival of managers on courses, problems of content and process identified in the previous chapter may be compounded into an irrelevant and perhaps deeply frustrating experience.

The processes of individual performance and potential review should be at the heart of an effective formal development scheme. The problems and opportunities involved in appraisal are now well known, are capable of being resolved, and are not peculiar to developing managers for the board. The problems of identifying potential are slightly less well identified and there is much less agreement on how they could be resolved. Rather than repeat these relatively well-ventilated arguments, effectively summarized in Randell,[2] it is more relevant to pick out aspects applying particularly to the directors we saw.

Appraisal was often mentioned by the organization as a significant management development tool, but was rarely mentioned by individual directors as having been influential on their development. (Nor indeed was there any suggestion it had been influential on their job performance.) While our interviews confirmed the relative ineffectiveness of many appraisal schemes, an even more important point was the extent to which past failure was compounded by present practice. Very few directors were themselves subject to appraisal in any significant sense. Even in organizations which had appraisal schemes, in which they themselves conducted appraisals of their subordinates, they were rarely reviewed formally by the Chief Executive or Chairman. These findings will probably not surprise anyone who has experienced what happens at the top of organizations. Nor will they be surprised by the absence of any discussion of whether directors themselves had development needs.

The reasons for the absence of such discussions are familiar. There is an implicit assumption that once you have arrived at main board level you are either fully equipped for the job you now do or are too senior for the issue to be discussed. Some directors told us that neither proposition was true in their case. They could see no logic in a system which required them to appraise their subordinates but refused them the same process with their boss; expressed the same views on the virtues of discussion about present and future that managers at all levels share; and said that just because they were on the board their need for and capacity to continue personal development had not ceased. While such comments were not made by all the directors we saw, they were made by a sufficient number to expose the failure of the system at the top level.

Some directors worked to written priorities and objectives agreed with the Chief Executive and had discussions with him. More frequently they existed in a top level environment where judgements about their performance were made on (as some of them saw) very large scale and often very vague criteria for what they were expected to achieve. Understandably directors, though being clear in many cases that this was unsatisfactory, were not necessarily in favour of a highly structured process that they might see as being applicable below them. But most of them, while having no ambition to take the final step to becoming a chief executive, saw the need for continued development in their existing jobs; new problems emerge, new needs have to be satisfied and the fact that you were fully experienced to do the job as it was last year did not mean that you have all the skills to do it this year. The processes by which this most important and potentially most productive area for improved formal development at the top could be improved are described in Chapter 13.

The case for Type 3 Development

Formal development processes, contrary to the occasionally cynical view of line managers, were not invented by personnel and management development specialists to provide themselves with something to do and to establish a position of power in the organization. They were designed to overcome the weaknesses of informal and accidental processes, recognizing that learning from experience was often insufficient and sometimes positively harmful in teaching the wrong lessons. The fact that some formal systems are not as successful as the designers would hope is not a reason for abandoning them. The improvement which can be made by Type 2 Management Development through normal job processes will still not be sufficient to provide people at the top with the skills and experience they need. Improved processes for learning through current experiences in Type 2 will not, for example, necessarily cover the longer term development of an individual or those aspects of management not encountered by managers in the current job. Formal development is part of the answer and has characteristics which make it uniquely appropriate for certain purposes. It therefore forms a desirable variant in management development which can be described as 'Type 3' Management Development (Figure 7.1).

Type 3 'Formal Management Development' – planned processes

Characteristics	– often away from normal managerial activities
	– explicit intention is development
	– clear development objectives
	– structured for development by developers
	– planned beforehand and reviewed subsequently as learning experiences
	– owned more by developers than managers
Development consequences	– learning may be real (through a job) or detached (through a course)
	– is more likely to be conscious, relatively infrequent

Figure 7.1 Type 3 Management Development

Managing for success

Formal management development processes would often be much more successful if they were properly managed, with effective design to meet the desired goals. They must meet consumer needs rather than those of the producer, and have not only general objectives but specific statements on outputs, and processes for measuring those outputs.

It was clear from our survey, from contact with a wide variety of organizations outside the survey and from reading management development literature that these requirements are insufficiently understood. One of the attractions of our survey to many of the participating organizations was that it gave them a process for measuring the effectiveness of their system, at least as it had applied in the past and for their most senior people. Figures 7.2 and 7.3 draw on the findings from the survey supplemented by other experience.

Clear appropriate job objectives
Effective selection for the job
Impetus from business opportunities/problems
Ownership of system shared:
    hierarchically, ie by line management
    by individual; self-development
    by personnel/training/management development
Development activities are:
    appropriate to need
    appropriate to individual
    based on management reality
Development processes are linked
Learning processes are identified and worked on
Outputs are identified and measured

Figure 7.2 Formal management development – levers for success

A number of these factors have already been discussed as general propositions and findings.

In Chapter 8 I shall be advancing the case for a contingent view of what effective management is. Generalized statements of what all good managers do are less valuable than specific statements of what particular managers in particular organizations ought to do. The general principles given above therefore need to be examined in each organizational context.

We need to see that the specific application of good principles may be easier and indeed more desirable in some organizations. Indeed Charles Handy[3] has argued that the processes of formal management development suit particular kinds of organizational culture better than it suits others. He argues that the standard processes of, for example, appraisal, planning and forecasting originated in what he describes as Role Cultures, and are appropriate to

Purposes:
  unclear
  unsupported by managers
Poor diagnosis of culture and business requirements
Poor analysis of individual needs
Development processes:
  unconvincing to managers
  inappropriate to need
  unreal
  unacceptable to individual
Over-emphasis on:
  formal
  general
  off the job
  future 'succession planning'
  mechanics
  one-off experiences
'Flavour of the month'
Owned by personnel/training

Figure 7.3 Formal management development – causes of failure

the kind of steady state organizations which develop Role Cultures. He suggests that such processes would actually be counter-productive in the other three cultures he identifies (Power, Task, Person). It is necessary to see his arguments in the context of his full description of those cultures in order to see how his comments apply in management development. One of the central points however is easy to grasp. Not only may the whole concept of management development be inappropriate in some organizations, but particular management development processes may fit well or badly.

An example derived from my own experience is that of self-appraisal. The idea of getting a manager to review his own performance in advance of a formal appraisal discussion, and contributing that review to the discussion, is attractive to many management development specialists. To introduce such processes into organizations in which the management processes are rigidly hierarchical, with very formal and untrusting relationships between bosses and subordinates, will be unsuccessful unless accompanied by other major revisions in management style.

Needs and development processes are linked like Siamese twins rather than being separate steps in a rational analytical process, as many management development systems imply. There can also be conflict between two different aspects of effective formal management development. Concentrating development on the current and future realities of management jobs has great attraction in terms of relevance and immediacy of payback. Planned development to meet an identified range of managerial skills is more effective than a casual approach based on the belief that all managers need the same kind of skills. However these priorities are in conflict with the fact that organizations and organizational demands change over the years. 'If we had known even ten years ago that our organization structure this year would be based on 15 profit centres, we would have set about producing managers capable of handling the profit centres. Our management development scheme was geared to a quite different sort of organization structure.' Concepts of effectiveness even within a function can change significantly; I know of several organizations which have dramatically changed their understanding of what the marketing function is about, and the same process may be happening in the personnel function. A scheme which may have been directly related to many of the aspects of 'Levers for Success' may cease to be relevant if it does not recognize changes as they occur even though it may not have been able to plan to meet them.

These illustrations show some of the problems of formal management development systems in the real managerial environment. Even if not overtly hostile, the real management world makes effective long term planning less productive than would be hoped. If for example a company has had a prolonged period of success it is unlikely to make use of formal processes which help managers to learn from the experience of adversity. Yet it is precisely the skills of dealing with adversity which will be needed if the company becomes less successful. Similarly organizations which have been created as or have become monopolies in a product or service are unlikely to have evolved formal management development processes for facing the harsh realities of competition. This does not mean that planning is impossible or not worth while. It suggests rather that there should be a decent level of humility about the likely results.

Managing careers

The general conclusion from our survey was that neither the organization nor the individual had in most cases managed careers, in the sense of a well-designed and well-implemented plan to take people to the top. This was partly because individual directors disclaimed long-term career ambitions of that kind, and partly that (as described earlier in the chapter) the planning processes for job rotation seem in most cases to have been absent or only partially implemented. Yet the planning of a career path would seem to be desirable from both an organizational and a personal point of view. In practice there seems to have been a shared unwillingness to focus on the issues involved in career planning, and to some extent a lack of the necessary tools to do so. Chapters 11, 12 and 13 give guidance on some of the processes which could be used to help individuals work on these issues. The two main essentials for effective career planning looking outwards from the individual are:

> a clearer understanding of individual values, types of satisfaction in work and in domestic life, and levels of skill and ability

> an awareness of opportunities in the existing organization and outside it.

As already indicated, the experience of most of the people we saw was that the organization failed on both counts. The evidence of our relatively small sample was confirmed by a variety of other sources. The requirements for effective organizational intervention in this process are spelled out particularly well by Hirsch[4]. She is helpful not only in identifying practical frameworks and processes but in describing the tensions and constraints which in practice inhibit neat career planning. One of the main reasons for problems is revealed in a different study[5] which showed that the number of managers spending their life with one organization had declined from 34 per cent in 1950 to 10 per cent in 1983. An important issue is whether top level management potential can be spotted very early, and whether this definition of potential will still be relevant by the time the high-flyer has reached the top. Organizations which believe the first may not have thought very much about the second, with the consequence that career planning is built not mererly with one shaky foundation, but two. Both these studies seem to reinforce the proposition that the individual must take responsibility for planning a career, not only because organizations may actually be bad at it, but because movement between organizations makes the contribution of any particular one less valid anyway.

Whereas the experience of many of our directors was that their moves within the organization had been unplanned by themselves and others, moves outside the organization were much more subject to the individual's own choice and indeed occasionally deliberate selection in advance rather than in response to a head hunter or a job advertisement. Again we find a conflict between different aspects of the process in which the managers then become involved. Variety of experience in a number of different organizations can be seen prospectively, and sometimes experienced, as of great assistance in the more senior jobs. Yet the decline in belief in the virtues of the professional general manager who can manage anything, expressed particularly through the work of John Kotter,[6] makes job-hopping perhaps less attractive both to organizations and individuals. For the individual however the amount of choice available within his or her current organization may determine whether a sensible career pattern involved moving outside it.

The problems of understanding and reconciling individual and organizational career planning needs are well described by Schein.[7] In terms of development for the top it is interesting to note that in his view the crisis, if it occurs, happens in mid career. This is the time when achievement compared to ambition, and the relative significance of work, career and the total life of the manager, may create enormous problems, which can be particularly traumatic if the needs of family and career conflict.

Promotion

Previous comments on career planning concentrated on matters of particular relevance to people who might be moving towards the top of organizations. It could be argued that a concern for planning the careers only of these people will be self-defeating and inefficient. Identification of and work for an élite minority will distance them from their fellows in a way which will not in the end produce effective managers at the top. In any case the process is inherently unreliable, in that some individuals identified will not make it to the top, while others not identified will.

Similar considerations apply to promotion decisions, and any attempt to manage them solely in order to produce better people at the top would be even more unrealistic. Career planning of course involves the possibility of moves which are not promotions; a manager may go into a different kind of job at the same level or the same job in a different organization as discussed in Chapter 2. The route to the top however involves promotion at some stage, even if it involves the owner's son being transformed from an untitled personal assistant into the Chief Executive.

The promotion process is fundamental within any organization for a variety of good immediate managerial reasons, but it is particularly crucial in relation to the formal managment development process. There is very little point in planning succession, drawing up development plans for individuals and putting people through development experiences if they are not then promoted to the position for which such processes are designed to equip them.

We did not study in our survey the selection processes by which the directors had been elevated to their current positions; indeed a number had been recruited from outside. Some organizations however described to us the ways in which their management development and planning system directly affected and probably improved the promotion processes. As one organization told us, collective widsom and collective pressure could be brought to bear. They had a committee which reviewed the development of individuals and had the right to comment on appointments. Although the line manager concerned still had the authority, his colleagues in the committee could comment on whether his prospective decisions were correct. Most importantly in the context of this book, comments were not based solely on the exhibited performance and personal characteristics of the manager, but on whether the manager's developmental experiences had included appropriate events.

The other aspect of this process, mirrored in a few other large organizations, was that of securing general agreement about senior management appointments. Whereas in some organizations the decision was made by the individual director acting entirely on his own, in a few this decision-making process was shared. This was particularly important not only because it increased the amount of information available about the individual, and sometimes its quality, but because it also brought into play the issues of the greater corporate good. Line directors if left alone to make their own decisions will naturally make the one which they think right in terms of their own self-interest; a promotion process which brings in colleagues facilitates decisions which may be equally right on the different criterion of corporate interest.

Promotion processes, like other selection processes, often have grave defects, the most significant of which is the failure to identify the requirements for effective performance in the job and the consequent requirements in the manager to fill it. Often the apparent successor is very visible, and hard thought on what needs to be done is low on the list of managerial priorities. In many organizations managers do not know the process used for determining promotion; is it simply decided by their boss or by their boss and his boss or by a committee? Nor do they know the criteria by which qualification for promotion is established. Some of the directors were very insistent that they had succeeded through hard work and a bit of luck, and that internal politics or being liked by someone important was not very relevant. No doubt such factors vary between organizations. There were however stories of people who had managed to create the right impression, or who were believed to be 'blue-eyed boys' rather than achieving through direct job performance. In my experience many managers will do their best to get round any formal promotion processes such as internal advertising and selection panels if they think they have exactly the right person for the job; such activities do not inhibit them from complaining if the same processes are applied to their disadvantage.

The obvious candidate for promotion may not be the right one in either the short or the long term. A management development or career planning system which does not address itself to the issue of making the right promotion decisions (particularly for the more senior jobs) is likely to fail.

Outsiders

The necessity to go outside for successors at board level may not imply a criticism of management development systems, which may have performed decently to meet previous expectations which have now changed. Organizations may go outside to attract skills and experience which they simply could not produce earlier.

The reasons why organizations go outside are less important for this book than the consequences. A belief in management development within the organization may suffer. A more personal consequence is that ousiders arrive with weaknesses as well as strengths. They are likely to be flawed in the sense that like everyone else they have high abilities in some areas and weaknesses in others. They will also have particular weaknesses in relation to the specific needs of their new business, expecially in terms of understanding the culture.

Outsiders are very often brought in, for example, to introduce a change which current executives either cannot or will not introduce. It is not at all clear that such attempts are generally successful, since, as we found in our survey, organizations are quite good at rejecting foreign bodies. One of the unstudied areas of management development is the absence of development action for many of these new arrivals, particularly at the most senior levels. Whether they have demonstrated the capacity to handle a new environment should be assessed as part of the selection process.

If their track record suggests that they can handle the new situation there is still a major development need not tackled by most organizations. At more junior levels it would be called the problem of induction. At senior levels it is the problem of providing the new entrant as quickly as possible with an understanding of the new environment, the different ways of doing things, the network, the powers and the influences which will largely determine success in the new job. The impact of such issues on job performance are well described in Gabarro and Kotter as shown in Chapter 2. It is an unnecessary risk to leave new directors, whose recruitment will have been expensive and the consequences of whose reduced performance will be even more expensive, to unplanned deep end experiences. New entrants of this kind ought to have a development programme prepared for and discussed with them, which should then be implemented and monitored over say their first six months in the new organization.

Individual management responsibilities

The term 'organization' is splendidly neutral. It is also slightly misleading in the sense that it is not really organizations which take action but individual managers. Managing management development on behalf of the organization is clearly influenced by the manager's attitude to the processes involved. One influence will of course be the manager's perceptions about the relevance of formal management development for his/her own personal development. Other influences on the manager's attitude are:

> Do I believe these processes will help; those being developed directly; me, indirectly?

> Are there any rewards for me in taking formal management development action?

> What is hurting in managerial performance under me that might be salved by such processes?

> Are there any punishments if I do not participate effectively?

> Where do these activities fit into the priorities which I feel to be right, and which my bosses exhibit?

> How relevant are the processes and the content of formal management development to managerial life as I know it?

Most managers understandably spend time where they have the option on activities which they enjoy and in which they are skilled. They do this in preference to undertaking activities which may actually be more important but which are less enjoyable and in which they feel less confident about their skills. It is not surprising therefore that since many of their responses to the questions indicated above do not support their involvement in formal management development, and they are required to behave as managers for this purpose differently from the way they behave in other aspects of managerial life, the attitude of many managers to management development as a formal process is often lukewarm.

On the other hand managers as they become more experienced grow more aware of what they need to do for themselves. If they have a boss who is not participating fully in the operational form of management development, they will find ways to get round the problem. If they think the management development system will not provide them with an answer they desire they will get round the system.

I was very interested in a job which I knew would be coming up in a different part of the organization in which I then worked. I knew the existing system would not consider me for it, nor would my boss put me up for it. I arranged to travel in a car with the divisional director concerned and without I think being blatant about it I showed an interest in the kind of thing which needed to be done and tried to show that I was a bright fellow. I got the job three months later.

I knew I had to get overseas experience if I wanted to get on, but I was told that I wouldn't get a look in unless I had production management experience. It was not in the interests of my boss to let me go, but I niggled away at him until I got a transfer to production. Eighteen months after that I went overseas.

This idea of self-initiated experience, in which the manager takes the responsibility for getting the responsibility, is very similar to the idea of self-development. Chapter 12 shows how the themes of self-development express the concept of management development as a process which is done by, rather than to, the individual. Self-development should be fully incorporated in formal management processes; it is a way of defining how the individual arrives at the appropriate development solution.

Early in this chapter I said the effectiveness of formal management development processes was contingent on the nature of the organization in which the development was to take place. It is in fact contintent upon a wide range of factors, which I have attempted to illustrate in the following chart (Figure 7.4). The first column, 'General contingent elements', focuses on influences essentially centred on the job. The third column looks at the factors

General contingent elements	Linking management development processes	Individual factors
– job content – organization structure – organizational climate – specific problems/ opportunities in management – business plans – rewards for development – history of management development – accident – boss/colleagues/ subordinates	– identifying needs and potential (individual) – reviewing organizational needs – planning to meet needs – individual and organzational – identifying development processes – selecting effective processes to meet – individual needs – organizational needs – identifying and using informal and formal development opportutunities	– recognition of need – identification of performance benefit – expectation of reward – past experiences – preferred learning style – learning skills – career plan – personal blockages – capacity to link tasks and learning – personal environment

Figure 7.4 Influences on management development within organizations

arising from the nature of the individual involved. Taken together the two columns show how many variable factors there are which will influence the effectiveness of any management development process, but perhaps most particulary formal organized Type 3 processes. In the middle column the management development processes which link the general and individual contingent factors are described. They are not links between specific items but apply generally across the two columns.

Managing all types of management development

Experience on the survey and our analysis of the results from it led to our development of the descriptive model of three types of management development. An earlier description of management development as an attempt to improve managerial effectiveness through a planned and deliberate learning process emerged as insufficient and inaccurate. Although I had written a book[8] which described how to make use of real management experiences as learning opportunities, I had not made the conceptual leap to create a new model of management development. The first six chapters of this book have now drawn up the essential elements of the model. I conclude this chapter with the complete model showing all three types (Figure 7.5).

I believe the model to be both conceptual and practical, in the sense that it is possible to identify immediately particular activities in real life. The necessity of drawing lines on a page contains the potential problem that people may see the types as wholly separate and mutually exclusive, and that is why the lines are drawn as wavy and slightly indeterminate. There are no high walls between the types. Type 2 is close to Type 1 in the sense that the same activity can be transformed by thought and planning from an accidental and not very efficient learning process into a more efficient one. Similarly the boundaries between Type 2 and Type 3 can be easily crossed. As suggested in Chapter 6 for example, courses designed specifically for learning purposes can nonetheless contain a very substantial element of reality. The Action Learning process is probably the best illustration of this. Here we have a combination of real work, normally on a project, in which however the prime purpose of the activity is to aid learning and development.

A well-managed management development process will therefore try to engage managers in all three types of management development, and will ensure that connections are established

Type 1 'Informal managerial' - accidental process

Characteristics
- occur within managerial activities
- explicit intention is task performance
- no clear development objectives
- unstructured in development terms
- not planned in advance
- owned by managers

Development consequences
- learning is real, direct, unconscious, insufficient

Type 2 'Integrated managerial' - opportunistic processes

Characteristics
- occur within managerial activities
- explicit intention both task performance and development
- clear development objectives
- structured for development by boss and subordinate
- planned beforehand or reviewed subsequently as learning experiences
- owned by managers

Development consequences
- learning is real, direct, conscious, more substantial

Type 3 'Formal management development' - planned processes

Characteristics
- often away from normal managerial activities
- explicit intention is development
- clear development objectives
- structured for development by developers
- planned beforehand and reviewed subsequently as learning experiences
- found more in developers than managers

Development consequences
- learning may be real (through a job) or detached (through a course)
- is more likely to be conscious, relatively infrequent

Figure 7.5 Model of types of management development

between them. One of the most effective ways of encouraging Type 2 management development will clearly be to show managers how learning activities in which they have been involved under the Type 3 label can be taken back and employed in the real world. Not only are such links a desirable and sensible feature of management development but one of the prime purposes of Type 3 management development should be to encourage precisely such a transfer back of learning opportunities. Type 3 processes ought not to centre solely on acquiring managerial techniques and managerial understanding, but ought to address more fundamentally the issue of enabling managers to learn better from their real world – to work through Type 2. If the processes used within type 3 development are indeed realistic then the objective I have just set also becomes realistic.

Summary

The elements of formal management development are now relatively well known. The idea that development for the most important decision-takers in an organization ought to be planned is effectively demonstrated as practical by some participants in our survey.

The actual processes used to identify needs and the failure to communicate plans to the individuals involved causes ineffectiveness. The tendency to create management development as a process apart from the reality of management is perhaps an even more potent generator of problems. Success lies both in improving the formal aspects of management development and in pursuing the integration of real management activities through both Type 2 and Type 3 processes.

References

1   Mant, A., *The Rise and Fall of the British Manager*, Macmillan, London, 1977
2   Randell, G., Staff Appraisal, IPM, London, 1984
3   Handy, C., *Understanding Organizations*, Penguin Books, London, 1985

4   Hirsch, W., *Career Management in the Organization*, Institute of Manpower Studies, Brighton, 1984
5   Alban-Metcalfe, B. and Nicholson, N., *Career Development for British Managers*, BIM, London, 1984
6   Kotter, J., *The General Managers*, Free Press, New York, 1982
7   Schein, E., *Career Dynamics*, Addison-Wesley, Reading, Mass., 1978
8   Mumford, A., *Making Experience Pay*, McGraw-Hill, London, 1980

Part II

Why Top Managers Learn

The nature of managerial work is different from what is implied by some of the theories which still dominate the content of much formal management development. The first chapters in Part II examine the nature of work at top level and the factors leading to different requirements in different organizations.

What directors actually do and what influences this are explored here at some length. This is done in order to illustrate to directors, and to those responsible for developing them, the variety of competencies which may need to be developed. The range of examples supports and extends the evidence given in the earlier chapters.

The last two chapters in Part II describe the learning processes involved and the individuality of the learner. They add a further dimension to the understanding necessary for effective development.

8 Development for what?

Earlier chapters have described the processes by which managers and directors learn and develop on their way to the top, and have shown why effective development processes centre on the reality of what managers do. Many of the development processes have of course been attached along the way, consciously or unconsciously, to the jobs currently being undertaken at the particular managerial level then occupied. Both before arriving at the top and after getting there, however, the development needs of individuals should ideally be assessed not just against some generalized view of what all 'good managers' need to be able to do well, but also against some view of the specific tasks and roles to be performed effectively at the top. In this chapter therefore the concern is to spell out what directors particularly need to be able to do well. A number of the requirements affecting managers at all levels have been put on one side. It is likely for example that all managers need to be able to carry out effective interviews, to communicate well, to set targets and monitor performance. Here we are concerned to look at those features of the director's job which are different from managerial jobs although not necessarily at a higher intellectual level as some authors have too readily described them

The classical view of management responsibilities

The first major writer on management, Henri Fayol identified five basic managerial functions – planning, organizing, co-ordinating, commanding and controlling. In various forms, usually by extending the number of present participles to include words such as staffing, directing and budgeting, this kind of description of what managers ought to do dominated the works of authors on management, students, and perhaps to some extent the analysis used by managers at work in formal job descriptions. While these descriptions have not entirely disappeared either from the literature (sometimes in more updated forms) or from organizational documents, serious thinkers have dismissed their significance in anything except an historical sense. It seems unlikely they were ever used by any significant number of managers as ways of carrying out their managerial work in practice. It is no doubt a commentary on the relative novelty, even in the United States, of the treatment of management as a serious process that the terms survived in the literature for so long.

The classical definitions are not helpful in providing guides for development purposes. At best they draw together a description of what an executive may be aiming to achieve; they do not describe what he does. If a director is holding a weekly management meeting, and discusses a particular problem with a supplier, he may be concerned with all of the processes described by Fayol. Managerial actions however are only usefully seen in more specific terms – the questions he asks, the way he involves people in the meeting. It is this specific behaviour which describes what the manager needs to do effectively and therefore what the development process should be aimed at.

The view held by managers themselves is, confusingly, not so much concerned with what managers do as what managers are. When asked to describe the skills or areas of effectiveness required for managers, a group of practitioners will most readily and enjoyably concoct a list of personal qualities, almost certainly defining them as leadership rather than managerial qualities. They will readily agree on a list including at least the following:

Decisiveness

Self-confidence

Enthusiasm

Trustworthiness

Courage

Sense of humour

Initiative

The vigour with which managers will generate a list like this is diminished to a more querulous response if they are asked to define what the words mean. One favoured word in the list above is 'initiative'. As one chief executive said to me, presumably without recognizing what he had said: 'I want people with guts and real initiative who will never give me any bad surprises.' He regarded my attempts to illustrate the problems of finding a manager who took initiatives without ever causing surprises with a relatively patient wish that I would get on with finding him.

The problem with lists of qualities of this kind, whether applied to junior management or directors, is that they are essentially descriptions of perceptions about things which surround the managerial activity rather than statements about what goes into it. In addition, for the purposes of this book they nearly all suffer from the great defect that even if you were able to define them in a way which meant something to most people, they are mostly qualities which are very difficult to influence through training or development. At this point of course some executives will leap up with a triumphant 'I told you so', feeling that I have confirmed what they have thought for years – that most important aspects of management are indeed unteachable. More considered reflection will perhaps indicate to them that although these aspects may be very important and may be unteachable, other aspects of what directors do are both definable and capable of being learned.

Skills, effectiveness and competence

An alternative to identifying extremely general words about management (the classical view) or the inherently vague descriptions of personal characteristics drawn from general discussion is to discuss with managers and directors what they actually do. Within organizations such discussions may be carried out by a training or management development specialist with a blank sheet of paper recording what managers think about their job content, or by providing checklists of desirable management processes or skills drawn from other organizations or perhaps from research. Research itself can be carried out at different levels of sophistication. I believe the most extensive and most thorough research has so far been carried out in the United States under the auspices of the American Management Association. Discussion and analysis with around 2000 managers at different levels and in different kinds of organization identified 18 characteristics or skills which all successful managers have in common. The research and its consequences have been written up by Boyatzis.[1]

Not the least important point about this list of competences is that it has been used to generate management development programmes by the AMA, thus producing a direct link between analysis and development which has been all too rare. This work is mentioned here because it provides a good basis for comparison with alternative definitions of what directors actually do. Boyatzis himself sets the most rigorous standards for the development of managers; whereas he believes much training is based on someone else's idea of what managers should know, he recommends that organizations should work from an explicit model of management tested in the organization. The 18 competences he describes can be used to define both the level of competence required in any particular job and the level of performance in that competence by individual managers. While at first sight he seems to be producing another generalized list of required skills and abilities, and indeed the 18 competences are said to be required by all successful managers, this view is qualified to the extent of saying that there will necessarily be variations of requirements in different organizations.

It is interesting to note that the most frequently purchased and perhaps the most widely read management best-seller of recent years, *In Search of Excellence*,[2] defined attractively what 'organizations' do, with extraordinarily little reference to what the people directing the organization have to do. Apart from colourful anecdotes about some dominating characters in their excellent companies, the authors do not describe what senior executives do or could do in order to manage the activities they describe as being necessary. While (as we will show in the next chapter) some of their conclusions have significance for our understanding of the context in which executives work and are developed, they are not helpful in meeting the concerns of this chapter.

We asked the participants in our survey what skills they thought necessary for the effective performance of the jobs they were doing. While this could have been an important survey in its own right, and therefore we did not pretend to be conducting a sophisticated analysis, some interesting and indicative points emerged. Perhaps the most interesting was that, as the members of the project team had experienced in other areas of our work, the people we were talking to were mostly not at all self-aware about the skills they actually needed. Experience with managers on processes such as writing job descriptions or helping with appraisal had already told us how difficult many managers find it to review their own job at all analytically. While the overall volume and quality of comment on the questions in our survey was not particularly exciting, the useful comments made were particularly significant because they were in the context of questions about development. In our view the responses were more meaningful in some respects precisely because the people we were interviewing were more conscious of things they needed to do well. Replies to questions put in another context might have slipped more readily into the kind of personal qualities approach indicated earlier. We selected the following as indicative of skills and behaviour which are *especially* necessary at board level:

> Identifying strategic direction
> Taking a corporate view rather than representing a functional division
> Absorbing and recalling quantities of data without losing sight of main issues
> Planning the future more than managing the present
> Managing external relationships
> Operating effectively in different organizational and national cultures
> Influencing directors as powerful as yourself
> Getting others to act rather than doing it yourself
> Relationships with non-executive directors

It will be noted that a number of these suggestions fit larger and perhaps multinational organizations more readily than smaller businesses with perhaps a single product or service.

Autobiographical revelations

It may well be that one of the required effectiveness areas of people at the top, not I think generally identified in the literature, is to be someone with strongly identifiable characteristics and priorities clearly recognized as operating in the business. Certainly it is my own experience from working in a variety of organizations that managers at all levels actually prefer to have one or perhaps two powerful individuals identified as the boss or 'the old man' who is seen to be driving the organization forward. While this is clearly much more true in private manufacturing and commerce than in public service (the civil service in general or organizations like the National Health Service), employees like to have someone at the top whose success they can admire. With the modern appetite of press and television for news about personalities, individuals can emerge as public figures beyond the intimate areas of their own success. Figures who 20 years ago would have been well known only within their own organization are now identified and trumpeted as exemplars of success to a wider public, the management component of which is apparently eager to be given the detailed recipe for what the successful top executives have done in creating or rescuing organizations.

If, like Lee Iacocca, you are able to write a book[3] which combines sustaining the success of one organization (Ford) and rescuing another (Chrysler) the attractiveness of your prescriptions extends over managers in organizations with a wide range between success and failure. Anecdotes about the personal habits of your ex-boss, while adding little to the managerial content of the book, may well add to its sales. It may say something about the state of the car industry everywhere outside Japan that the rough equivalent of Iacocca's book is that of Sir Michael Edwardes,[4] more limited in the sense that it does not deal with experience in two big companies, and more time-bound in the sense that Sir Michael's rescue act seems now to have been a temporary halt in an apparently permanent decline.

Of course such books contain nuggets about the management process at all sorts of level, and give at the top examples of managing or attempting to manage the external environment. Managers who followed Iacocca's prescription of setting personal priorities, not working at weekends and having a three-month review of objectives and plans might find their managerial and personal life improved. The books are genuinely helpful in that they provide a view of the variety of pressures on top executives. Beyond that they are not likely to add to an understanding of top level jobs and of performance within those jobs, not least because the kind of public self-justification at the core of these books represents only a partial truth.

It is interesting to compare modern autobiographies with the first and to many people the greatest, that of Alfred P Sloan.[5] While, in showing how excellent had been his stewardship of General Motors over 40 years, he is by no means immune from the same desire for glory, there does seem to be a substantial difference of purpose in this book. Sloan was attempting to describe the processes of management which he had developed and successfully deployed over many years, and to analyse the reasons why he introduced them, rather than to justify particular decisions and what he said to whom over what issue in the novelettish way familiar from our modern giants. While there is far more substance in Sloan's book, it is much more useful as an historical survey of the development of management practices than as a guide to current realities in management. While some things have remained the same, there are staggering gaps in his book in terms of present requirements. For example, while he describes his personal involvement in selection processes in a way which is fascinating although not necessarily a good guide for similar involvement for other chief executives, he has nothing to say in the issues of central government and the external environment which bulked so large in Iacocca and Edwardes. From the point of view of this book it is also particularly relevant to see that issues of succession and development were not part of his concerns.

Not only are these books lacking (except for Sloan's) an organized view of the management processes which might help us for this chapter, they must also be read with caution in terms of accuracy of perception. Reviewers have told us that there are different stories about the precise contribution of Iacocca in certainly Ford and perhaps Chrysler. We have not seen the alternative view expressed at equivalent length. We do know however from analogies with other forms of autobiography that a reliance on one person's statement of what he does, how he does it, with what objectives and with what results must be treated with caution. The obvious analogy is with the world of politics, where it is for example possible to compare the stories of Harold Wilson and George Brown about the same managerial episodes in government.

It is also possible to draw an analogy from the sporting world from which leadership comparisons are sometimes drawn. Here we have the advantage of the considered study by Mike Brearley of *The Art of Captaincy*,[6] as well as his earlier narratives of his great successes. This is the man admiringly proclaimed by an Australian rival as having a degree in people as an explanation of how he had manipulated or, as we would say in business, 'managed' his team to success. We have however another version[7] from the slow bowler Phil Edmonds, who was not responsive to Brearley's processes. Edmonds has a different story about the interaction between them and why it was unsuccessful. While, like some aspects of the Iacocca and Edwardes stories, this has its novelettish fascination, its more substantial significance is that stories of the great by the great are not necessarily properly representative either of what they do or of the results of what they do.

I have gone to some trouble over these autobiographical stories because of their popularity and because they seem significantly misleading about jobs at the top. I am not saying they should not be read; I am suggesting careful evaluation of what they actually mean.

Leaders or managers

There is undoubtedly confusion between these two words. Partly the confusion arises because of the need to describe people who are furthering the purposes of an organization but who are not normally seen as managers. Thus someone like the Archbishop of Canterbury might be seen to have amongst other things a leadership role within the Church of England, within which in the 1980s he might conceivably recognize that he operates sometimes as a manager. Similarly in the armed services leadership is a required quality and it would tend to be regarded as the more significant aspect of the work of people-directing activities, rather than the managerial processes which might similarly be involved in planning and organzational work. In industrial and commercial life the managerial process would normally be regarded as the more significant, leadership being a required element within it. Leadership would then be seen as the capacity to influence others to get things done, and when researchers began to look at the processes involved in getting other people to act, the terms of leadership style and management style became effectively interchangeable.

Leadership is undoubtedly an important term to many managers and in the perception of what people at the top of organizations are supposed to provide. As we have shown in the previous section, there is obviously a strong need to identify a dominant character, which seems to be true from shop-floor level to the very top of the organization. While this need might have been constant, specific attention to the leadership process has fluctuated over the last 40 years. An initial drive after the 1939-45 war, pursuing rather super-ficial analogies with the recent achievements of the armed services, was followed by a period in which these analogies were decried. The military connection reappeared with the work of John Adair, whose original investigations on the subject through his work as a lecturer in the army became extended into a much wider study of leadership in many different spheres of life. His view of the leader is one of three interlocking circles which he describes as

   Achieving the task

   Building the team

   Developing the individual

The most readily available and cheapest of his many books on this subject is *Effective Leadership*.[8] In many ways his list of leadership skills is similar to the classical management list mentioned at the beginning of this chapter, and indeed it includes a number of the same words. His work is a good illustration of the point that statements about leadership can be seen to apply outside the indus-trial and commercial field; but the most identifiable parts of his leadership concept are essentially managerial.

A number of people clearly like to have someone they see as superior to themselves who can be described as 'the leader'. Equally some executives and managers like to cast themselves in this role and place a gloss on their activities by describing them as leadership roles. When however we try to distinguish between leadership and managerial activities, it seems that the definable things are all managerial and we are left with a residue of descriptions nearly always personal and qualitative in nature such as 'inspires trust'. The attempt of Zaleznik to describe managers and leaders as different people[9] works only by following him into the realm of psychological types, and by accepting his view that desirable issues such as imagination and creativity are leadership and not managerial activities, or rather are possessed by one psychological type who becomes the leader and not by another type who can be an effective manager.

The potency of the word and the concept remains. This can be seen in the continued popularity of books and the attractiveness of some courses, often based on an outdoor experience, which include the word leadership in the title. Perhaps the vagueness and yet the attractiveness of the word necessarily go together. It is unlikely that people will cease to want somebody they call a 'leader'. It is unlikely that people at the top of organizations will cease to enjoy being called leaders. It seems even less likely that anything will emerge about the processes of leadership which will be sufficiently differentiated from the processes of effective management to provide any substantial clues on behaviour which would lead to effective development processes.

Reality in management – research

The supposedly ideal picture drawn by classical theorists would, if it existed, apply most clearly at the top level of any organization. Of the four important pieces of research which demolished the classical view as a useful picture three are studies taken at the top of organizations. Indeed the very first study by the Swede Carlson[10] was on managing directors. The research workers used four processes to establish reality – self-completed diaries, questionnaires, interviews and observation, used in different proportions by each. The essential point differentiating these studies from those discussed earlier, and of course from theoretical or anecdotal material drawn from very little data, is that the material has been produced by studying what actually happened and analysing the material systematically, reaching conclusions only where they can be supported by empirical evidence.

Rosemary Stewart's work [11,12] is by far the most comprehensive in terms of the length of time over which she has been conducting research and the number of managers involved, which now runs into hundreds. While her evidence is clearly the most weighty and conclusive, simply because of the volume, it does not deal specifically with the top level. Her conclusions are however so important, and share so much with the original earth-breaking study by Carlson, that the main features are summarized here:

> Managers do not work according to the neat well-organized themes of the classical management school.

> Their activities are characterized by brevity, variety and fragmentation.

> They spend most of their time interacting with other people rather than thinking well-organized thoughts.

> They work at a brisk and continuing pace with little free time.

> So far from being subject to extremely generalized comments about 'what all managers do' there is a substantial variety in the objective demands of managerial jobs.

> In addition to objective differences, for example between a sales manager and a research manager, personal choices are made by managers which affect what they actually do.

Managers often experience their jobs as being controlled by demands placed upon them or contraints around them and recognize too little the choices which they have actually made or could make. These differences of choice are not to be simply expressed in terms of management style, for example whether to be directive or consultative, but in terms of the actual content of what the job holder chooses to do. These conclusions are substantially shared with all the researchers mentioned here, although each has a different subsequent model for interpreting what managers do.

Chronologically the next major researcher following Carlson and Stewart was Henry Mintzberg.[13] The challenge he was offering to accepted views of managerial processes is better indicated by and more accessible in his *Harvard Business Review* article 'The manager's job, folklore and fact'.[14] He collected his data by observing five chief executive officers at work, rather than getting them to complete diaries. In contrast with the view of the manager as a reflective systematic planner, working through formal management information, he confirmed many of the views expressed above by Rosemary Stewart. But whereas Stewart tended to draw out differences and the reasons for them in the performance of managerial jobs, Mintzberg was struck by essential similarities which he thought outweighed differences, though he saw the latter as being important. He applied contingency theory to them saying that performance was influenced by:

> the organization itself, the industry and factors in the environment
> factors in the job itself
> the impact of the job holder in personality and style
> current situational factors, perhaps relatively temporary issues.

He found his executives working at an unrelenting pace, with the same brevity, variety and fragmentation identified by Stewart. They had a substantial preference for live action, by which he meant activities that are current, specific and well defined and possibly non-routine: 'time to think' was less popular. A great proportion of time was spend in oral communication which was much preferred to letter writing. Personal face-to-face contact was thought to be the best process, as assessed by the time actually spent on it. Executives had a wide variety of contacts with superiors, subordinates and outsiders.

Mintzberg's identification of the essential similarity within managerial jobs was carefully qualified by the contingent factors identified above. The similarities are expressed by him in terms of ten roles, as shown opposite.

While proposing that all managers exercise each of these roles, Mintzberg recognizes that different managers will give different priorities to them, presumably using the aforementioned contingency analysis.

Apart from its fundamental importance as analysis of what senior executives did from his observation of them, Mitzberg's role description is of substantial value for developmental purposes. It is an analysis which can readily be used by managers to look at their own jobs, for example by rating the roles in terms of the priorities they accord and the time they spend. This in turn can lead to a discussion as to whether the allocation of priority and time is approp-

a) *Interpersonal roles*
   Figurehead
   Leader
   Liaison

b) *Informational roles*
   Monitor
   Disseminator
   Spokesman

c) *Decisional roles*
   Entrepreneur
   Disturbance handler
   Resource allocator
   Negotiator

riate and if not what ought to be done about it. The consequence in developmental terms may be a discussion of the kind of skills that an executive needs to carry out the role, the lack of which sometimes brings about the apparent low priority accorded to any particular aspect.

In case it should be thought that Mintzberg has merely replaced one set of five or ten words with another, it is important to emphasize that in each case he offers a description of content of the role which provides a direct test in terms of particular behaviour for any manager interested to assess what he is doing or what he needs to do in future.

The next contributor to our understanding of requirements in top jobs was John P Kotter.[15] Interestingly some of the results and ideas in this book were partially previewed in a similarly small-scale study of local government top executives.[16] His study of 15 general managers was not exclusively about the single top job holder but of executives in general management jobs holding positions with some multifunctional responsibility for a business or businesses. Some of them were subsidiaries of larger corporations, and were therefore unlike the vast majority of directors in my own study, but clearly like senior executives in many organizations. They are however apparently more like Mintzberg's chief executives, in the sense that they manage a range of functions, than the wide range of funtional managers reported by Stewart. Kotter undertook an intensive study of these individuals, taking about one month in total over each participant and including observation, interviews, questionnaires and the collection of relevant documents. He found that general managers were not:

strategic
reflective
proactive
well organized

The explanation was on-the-job demands which he identified as:

setting goals in conditions of uncertainty
allocating resources in relation to competing claims
problem solving of three kinds
    firefighting
    looking at the causes of problems
    identifying solutions
organizing informal co-operation
implementing decisions rather than making them
motivating and controlling large groups of subordinates

Like Mintzberg he saw these as constant demands applying to all general managers but the influence of them was different in intensity and effectiveness. While these managers were, compared to the textbooks, neither well organized nor systematic in their approach to the management task, he found three characteristics of effective behaviour:

developing an agenda (often different from a 'plan')
building networks involving
    bosses, colleagues, subordinates and outsiders
    rewards given to secure desired behaviour in others
    establishing values and norms
execution
    establishing multiple objectives
    maintaining relationships
working through meetings and dialogues
spending time with others

The following additional aspects are important:

They engage in a wide range of discussions with many different people, and the issues under discussion are not necessarily top management issues.

They ask a lot of questions.

Big decisions are extremely rare.

Discussions are not focused exclusively on business issues but involve joking and non-work-related discussion.

The substantive issue discussed is sometimes unimportant to the business.

Executives rarely give orders in a traditional sense.

They frequently engage in attempts to influence others by asking, requesting, cajoling, persuading and even intimidating.

They react to other people's initiatives in allocating their time and much of their day is unplanned.

They work long hours.

They respond to having to decide what to do despite uncertainty, great diversity and vast amounts of apparently relevant information by a process he calls 'agenda setting'. This is less explicit than the formal planning process and indeed often includes items outside the plans.

Their process for achieving these agendas involves allocating significant time and effort to developing a network of co-operative relationships amongst the people who will help them to achieve the agendas. They then use the components of the network in implementation. Sometimes they do so by direct influence, sometimes by indirect processes where the message is got across by a variety of methods.

Kotter created a stunningly significant concept – the efficiency of seemingly inefficient behaviour. The fact that executives rarely plan their days in advance in much detail but rather react to the day's needs through conversations that are short, disjointed and often deal with a variety of issues in the space of a few minutes is seemingly inefficient. It is precisely this kind of inefficient behaviour which it is often proposed to tackle by suggestions that managers should plan their day more, should control their time, should be less responsive to the pressing needs of those around them. Kotter's observation was that the apparently accidental and often opportunistic way in which general managers operate is actually efficient, because it provides essential information, understanding and contact. While being responsive to the needs of others they can direct their attention to issues on their personal agenda highlighted by apparently accidental experiences.

In development terms Kotter is explicit about the implications for career movement training and education programmes. Firstly he found that the majority of successful general managers were people who knew the business and the people involved, and that the concept of a professional manager moving around between businesses and particularly between industries is probably very unsound. Growing your own executive is therefore not only an alternative to going outside to recruit perhaps seemingly more professional managers, but is in all probability a less risky and costly operation; 'home-grown' executives acquire knowledge and experience which so-called professional experience outside does not provide. Secondly Kotter suggests that management training and education courses probably over-emphasize unambiguous problems, formal tools and over-simplistic skill processes dealing with human relationships.

Isenberg[17] develops some of Kotter's findings from his own analysis through a similarly detailed collection of information from a very few senior managers. He emphasizes that they have to deal with the context of ambiguity, inconsistency and surprise, and that they do so by managing a network of interrelated problems rather than neatly identifiable and separate ones. They use intuition which he defines as the ability to sense when a problem exists. He is careful to say that it is not the opposite of rationality or an excuse to be capricious. He says that managers tend not to think too much about a problem unless they sense it is solvable.

One response to all these findings is that managers ought to be better organized, more systematic, more rational, more controlled in the allocation of their time. All these authors would argue however that while they are not proposing the abolition of rationality, sense and organization in management processes some of the seeming inefficiencies are less inefficient, at least some of the time, than they appear; and that many of the processes described here are a necessary and inevitable part of the real nature of management. From a development point of view the central message is that it is possible to describe and analyse processes which do not fit the managerial textbooks but which actually produce good results. Such development processes can be geared to the actual needs of managers – to learn for example how to define an agenda and manage networks, and the processes of influencing people.

My own experiences of working as an employee in a variety of different organizations, getting closer to the top and the top people, substantially confirms the findings of the researchers. My views are summarized in Figure 8.1, and I can identify at top level some additions to Mintzberg's list.

Hectic Pace

Fragmented Behaviour

Is More	*Is Less*
Intuitive	Rational
Responsive	Reflective
Unaware	Sensitive
Unplanned	Proactive

Processing Information –
Often Unprogrammed

Use of Informal Networks

Interactive

Multi-programmed

More Often Constrained Than Innovative

Specific and Contingent
– on nature of job
– on perceptions and preferences of individual

Figure 8.1 Reality in management

Challenging the culture

First, the capacity of managers to identify the issues involved in demands, choices and constraints as described by Rosemary Stewart. My career has covered industries as diverse as magazine publication, construction, computers and chemical engineering. My experience with directors in those businesses was that important though the industrial context was, by far the most significant factor was the capacity to break out of the personal and organizational mould which the culture and the nature of the business seem to impose. The ability of senior managers to recognize what is meant by 'that's the way things are around here' and to balance acceptance of and challenge to this seems to me the process by which an organizational effort is transformed. These issues and the implications for development are discussed at greater length in the next chapter.

Teams

The research literature reviewed here makes practically no reference to teams. Do top managers need to work in teams? It may seem obvious that a board ought to be a team, but this may be too easy an assumption. Not only was the actuality of several boards that I have experience different, but this actuality represented what the organization wanted. If top management wants to act as a team there are understandings and skills expressed for example by Belbin[18] and Margerison[19] which will help to identify particular individual contributions. Some businesses however are not run as corporate activities and therefore the team issue may not present a legitimate director function at that particular level, although it may do so at lower management levels. Some businesses are run, want to be run and ought to be run with separate functions or geographical divisions with no significant requirements for a team to reach general agreement on the activities of the organization. In these cases, as Casey shows,[20] the simplistic assumption that all managers need to work effectively in teams may certainly be untrue at the top.

Inefficiency *is* sometimes inefficient

My own experience also suggests that the researchers, in their understandable and helpful desire to reinterpret apparently inefficient managerial behaviour as efficient, have perhaps underplayed the extent to which a lot of top management behaviour is unnecessarily inefficient. Of course top executives will be faced with unplanned and unforeseen events. But to see as I have done the crisis-ridden reaction to a lost order, to the sudden departure of a top executive, to bad figures for one month's trading, was both illuminating and saddening. It is not simply that 'the situation' demands that top managers respond to such events in an unreflective response more driven by the need for action than calm consideration. It is rather too often that a manager who shows signs of wishing to think through a problem carefully is perceived as indecisive and not on top of the job, unwilling to take responsibility.

Even at the most senior levels, where the longer term and strategic vision is generally identified even by managers themselves as being desirable, there was a substantial gap between what would have been effective performance and actual performance. In fact there were two kinds of gap. Where managers did indulge in planning for tomorrow, too often the planning was unrealistically optimistic, lacking an awareness of the competitive issues and potential changes in the environment, and most particularly lacking careful thought about how the plan would be implemented. A second gap occurred during an organization's less successful periods when planning would disappear entirely and managerial activities even at the top because of a process of excusing yesterday instead of managing tomorrow. This is a critical failure because unless top management plans ahead the effective imperatives lower down the organization will certainly ensure that no one else does.

Travel

The process of networking identified by both Mintzberg and Kotter is certainly crucial. One of the aspects of this not mentioned by them is that of travel. Networking is effective only if it is sustained by a wide range of contacts, not merely those with main board colleagues which might seem to be most important. This in many companies will involve travelling over the country, a continent or the world. The studies of executive time have taken this insufficiently into account. It is not simply the fact of time spent away from the office, and the possible results in terms of effective networks. It is rather that the nature of travel and its consequences may change at top level. The significance and challenge of contacts necessary for effectively managing other people through infrequent visits, often after or during travel processes which are extremely tiring, place additional demands on the top executive. These demands are more than those mentioned in the next chapter of understanding differing cultures whether organizational or national. Meeting them effectively does not occur naturally but must be subject to effective personal development.

While some authors on management have identified the difference between operational and strategic skills, commenting (like some of the participants in our survey) on the greater need at top management level for the latter, the need for an effective combination has been insufficiently understood. As the writers who have understood reality have commented, people at the top have to respond to unplanned and immediate problems and therefore must have immediate operational skills. They also need strategic and visionary skills because without them the organization is likely to drift, pushed and battered by crises and perhaps the effective action of competitors. While one answer if we made the team analogy would be to ensure that each team of top managers has a proportion of people equipped with each kind of skill, operational and strategic, it would seem both more realistic and more effective if each top level manager were equipped with each set of skills.

One answer by many organizations including several in which I worked was to identify particular periods of the year as those in which strategic thinking was allowed, encouraged or indeed even demanded. But the nature of what occurs in management requires more frequently a combination of the two skills during the whole year. Top managers need to deploy their immediate tactical operational and firefighting skills within an understanding and use of strategic issues and decisions. The separation of the two has in my experience led to failures at the operational level and a waste of time in terms of strategic planning and decisions never actually implemented. Again it is a question of not separating management into boxes which are intellectually comprehensible but do not relate to the demands of management in practice.

Change

I will be describing in the next chapter some of the processes and the context required for the effective implementation of change. As

Kanter[21] has shown, a variety of factors decide whether an organization becomes successful in introducing innovation. The personal responsibility of top management for understanding these factors and the need for innovation is particularly important, expecially as it is unlikely to be tackled successfully purely as an internal process. Top managers must spend time in working out how to shift their products, processes and services from their current position, even though successful, to a new position – the inevitable requirement for progress. In Kanter's view the three new skills required are those of persuading others to invest information, support and resources in new initiatives; managing the problems associated with the greater use of teams and employee participation; and understanding how change is designed and constructed in an organization.

Ethics

The way top management behaves substantially determines the ethical conduct of what the organization is attempting to achieve. Supplier/purchaser relationships, desired forms of behaviour to employees, the processes of dealing with environmental issues – all these are processes which while not peculiar to top management are necessarily defined by them. A fascinating Granada TV series, 'Business Decisions' in 1982, showed both the dilemmas and the evasions involved for top management. It seems easier in many organizations to ignore the issues and hope they will go away rather than try to manage them. Increased public attention directed at companies which have failed to manage these issues indicates that evasion is not a long-term answer.

John Harvey-Jones, Chairman of ICI, said in a lecture at the Royal Society of Arts in 1984: 'You cannot in industry work totally on the principle that the end justifies the means. The ends have to be felt to be good and the ethics of the organization, ie how it behaves in pursuit of its ends, have to be also seen to be decent and in tune with the times.'

We shall be looking in the next chapter at the many influences on what top managers do, including the nature of the organization and its purposes. In this chapter we have looked at the things they do which create the need to learn. We have seen how top managers establish processes, not necessarily clear to themselves, for review-ing and understanding what is happening in their organization. The capacity to assess current policies and the effectiveness of current managerial actions extends beyond the influence of any individual to the success of the organization itself. Where managers undertake these reviews successfully they are able to redefine the purposes of the organization to meet new challenges or to meet a different perception of the organization's purposes. The capacity of the top group of managers not only to ensure that they themselves are equipped to deal with the management problems with which they are familiar, but also to challenge the ways in which those management problems are defined and perceived, seems to be a rare but desirable attribute. This capacity can be seen for example in organizations which have historically been production orientated turning themselves into marketing orientated organizations. The organizational learning process has been that of redefining current success in meeting traditional policies and objectives and recogniz-ing that the success is insufficient or will not last. This type of learn-ing challenge is discussed, with special reference to the work of Argyris, in Chapter 11.

A look at the future

Any picture of what top managers currently do is likely to be at least partially misleading about how future top managers should be developed, in that new opportunities and challenges emerge not only within individual organizations but perhaps affecting a large number of organizations. Forecasting is of course risky, and this is especially true in the area of management where forecasts about changes in the requirements placed on managers depend in turn on changes in the environment, in society and in technology which are themselves forecasts. The most likely changes in the requirements of what top managements should do seem to be:

Organization structure

Just as the matrix was the great structural revolution of the 1970s, and was essentially a process demanded in some organizations by technology and in others by service to customers, other changes in technology may lead to yet further forms of organization structure. Changes in the technology of communication may make less necessary those elements of autonomy in managerial behaviour presently caused by physical separation of units. This would suggest contradictory pressures, technology facilitating more centralization in conflict with a growing belief that small units with specific managerial responsibility are good for clients or customers and for managers.

Independent workers

We have already seen the development, for example in F International in the United Kingdom, of employment processes enabling brain workers to stay at home rather than appear at a central location. There are associated developments where less reliance is placed on full-time permanent expertise being available in the organization and more on securing it when required from part-time workers or from consultants. The problems of managing people who rarely meet, have perhaps no prime identification with the organization which they serve, no shared values, and who are not subject to some of the normal managerial constraints and disciplines will certainly produce requirements for more sophisticated top management processes.

Conflicting objectives

We have seen in the 1980s in the United Kingdom a sharp move towards the identification of apparently clear economic or profit goals, with less attention to the social consequences of their pursuit. While in some industries this has made the task of managers apparently more simple, in others the conflict between economic and social pressures remains, for example in the nuclear industry. Western culture tends towards simple goals, clear and direct responsibilities and the assertion of managerial power. Tolerance of ambiguity may well be more present in Japan but may also emerge in at least some organizations in the Western world.

Minority groups

Meeting the aspirations, and indeed helping those concerned to define the aspirations, of women and non-white groups in the working population seems likely to become a factor which the almost entirely white (and male) top management population will not be able to ignore. Amongst the many issues involved is the fact that the vast majority of managers lack at the moment the capacity either to understand the problem or to manage the relationships involved effectively.

Conclusions

From this analysis, the basic conclusion for the development of top managers is clear. The prime focus ought to be on what they actually do rather than on generalized ideas of what managers ought to do. Attention must be paid to the needs of individual managers in individual organizations. The mechanics of this may be achieved satisfactorily through, for example, the use of Mintzberg's role analysis. While the statements of roles are themselves generalized, a process can be set up through which top management identifies which roles have primacy in their particular organization, which in turn can lead to an assessment of current individual skills and therefore of development needs. Alternatively organizations can generate their own form of analysis by drawing together the material suggested here from a wider variety of sources.

It is not simply a matter of identifying a particular management skill relatively widely used already by personnel and management training people. The problem with identifying skills through such current processes as training needs analysis or appraisal is that the skills tend then to be identified and worked on as separate individual processes. While convenient from a teaching point of view this has the disadvantage of being unrealistic in terms of what a manager actually does. Interviewing skills, for example, are taught most frequently as a discreet selection activity, less often as a connected series of skills deployed in similar formal occasions such as appraisal and counselling. While it is necessary and desirable that managers should have the skills for these formal occasions, the more realistic position is that managers deploy them in a much wider and more informal series of activities. Managers spend a great deal of their time collecting information from other people in their normal managerial work, for example in reviewing performance against budget or asking questions about a subordinate's plans for the next three months. The very sensible pursuit of skills in relation to the more easily defined processes (often incidentally defined that way because personnel people do the defining) is necessary but not sufficient for understanding the reality of managerial life.

The fact brought out by Kotter, Mintzberg and Stewart is that the structured systematic neatness proposed by many past managerial theorists not only has no connection with what managers currently do, but has no sensible connection in many circumstances with what managers ought to do. The task therefore is not simply to help managers set up and manage neat managerial processes (although many of these processes could benefit from being better organized) but to help them manage better the confused reality of management. It is especially true that courses as development activities suffer because they do not sufficiently encounter this confused reality. Not only is the content all too often insufficiently aware of the analyses offered in this chapter, but the process itself, by placing activities in discreet boxes, further distances this learning experience form the reality in which the manager works.

References

1   Boyatzis, R., *The Competent Manager*, Wiley, New York, 1982
2   Peters, T. and Waterman, R., *In Search of Excellence*, Harper & Row, New York, 1983
3   Iacocca, L., *Iacocca*, Sidgwick & Jackson, London, 1985
4   Edwardes, M., *Back From The Brink*, Collins, London, 1983
5   Sloan, A., *My Years With General Motors*, Penguin Books, London, 1986
6   Brearley, M., *The Art of Captaincy*, Hodder & Stoughton, London, 1985
7   Barnes, A., *Phil Edmonds*, Kingswood, London, 1986
8   Adair, J., *Effective Leadership*, Gower/Pan, 1983
9   Zaleznik, A., 'Managers and Leaders: Are They Different?', *Harvard Business Review*, May/June 1977, pp. 67–77

10 Carlson, S., *Executive Behaviour*, Strombergs, Stockholm, 1951
11 Stewart, R., *Contrasts in Management*, McGraw-Hill, London, 1976
12 Stewart, R., *Choices for the Manager*, McGraw-Hill, London, 1982
13 Mintzberg, H., *The Nature of Managerial Work*, Prentice-Hall, Englewood Cliffs, New Jersey, 1980
14 Mintzberg, H., 'The manager's job, folklore and fact', *Harvard Business Review*. July/Aug. 1975, pp. 49–59
15 Kotter, J.P., *The General Managers*, Free Press, New York, 1982
16 Kotter, J.P. and Lawrence, R., *Mayors in Action*, Wiley, New York, 1974
17 Isenberg, D.J., 'How senior managers think', *Harvard Business Review* Nov./Dec. 1984, pp. 81–90
18 Belbin, R.M., *Management Teams*, Heinemann, London, 1981
19 Margerison, C. and McCann, A., *How to Lead a Winning Team*, MCB University Press, Bradford, 1985
20 Casey, D. and Critchley, W., 'Team building' in A. Mumford, *Handbook of Management Development*, Gower 1986
21 Kanter, R.M., *The Change Masters*, Simon and Schuster, New York, 1983

9 Influences on managers – within the organization

The previous chapter discussed ways of looking at top management jobs. What managers do was described as both contingent upon the job itself and the situation in which the job is performed, and dependent on the personal preferences, experience and interests of the job holder. These job factors have the most powerful and direct effect on the required content of development for top jobs.

In this chapter we will consider a wide range of less immediate influences on what managers at the top do, such as the organization's objectives and the priorities of the chief executive. These aspects, with those covered in the previous and next chapters, determine what the director has to do and how it is done – and therefore set not only the development requirements but also the context within which development does or does not take place. Understanding of these factors is vital if development is to be related to the actuality of the organization.

The intention here is to concentrate on those influences which apply at the top and at the level immediately next to it, even though in some respects they may also have affected the managers throughout their career in the organization. In addition, the emphasis is on those factors which directly influence personal development rather than other aspects of a manager's working life.

How people at the top form their jobs is the result of immediate pressures and past history, as applied to the organization and to the individual within it. The individual struggles to survive, to redifine objectives and tasks, to seek new opportunities or different ways of overcoming problems. The capacity of the manager to do this is substantially influenced by successful personal experience of struggle, by new encouragement and input offered by the environment at large or by particular individuals within the organization, or indeed by particular development experiences specifically designed to help the individual understand what might be achieved. A manager might be influenced for example by reading John Kotter or Rosemary Stewart. An external course, or a chance meeting with a successful manager outside the immediate organization, might provide a stimulus.

The struggle of the individual takes place however within a context of a larger whole; the organization, its present and its past. The struggle takes place within the organization's own environment, but is subject to influences from outside that environment and by substantial factors around the individual representing strong forces in life rather than individual differences at a micro level. The interaction is shown in Figure 9.1.

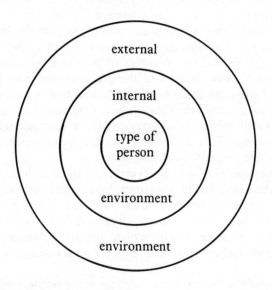

external

internal

type of
person

environment

environment

Figure 9.1 Types of influence

Organizational culture and structure

The argument about the balance between nurture and nature – the extent to which we are the product of our genes or of our environment – is familiar to most of us, not least as parents. As the schoolgirl criticized by her parents for a poor school report commented, 'Do I blame heredity or environment?' What managers do, what they demonstrate themselves to be, and their capacity to develop themselves and be developed are influenced in a variety of ways by the environment in which they work.

Formal statements

It would seem natural to look first at the material provided by the organization to guide the top manager. This may be a job description, a set of objectives, a series of priorities. It was interesting during our survey to get confirmation of previous experience. Few of our directors seemed to have an up-to-date statement of what their job was or what they were supposed to achieve in anything except financial terms. Some organizations clearly believe in specific job descriptions, produced even for the top jobs and sometimes updated regularly. Other organizations would regard such written documents as irrelevant and bureaucratic intervention, since either you know what you are supposed to do once you've reached the top, or alternatively jobs at the top are by their nature indefinable.

The potentially most significant statement about what managers do may well therefore be lacking in many organizations. What people at the top do is in practice subject, certainly in these latter cases and sometimes even when a job has been spelt out clearly in terms of priorities and objectives, to a variety of immediate pressures, circumstances of a short-term nature and a mixture of longer-term and often historical factors.

The word culture would be understood by thinking managers to be a description of deep-set common beliefs and practices within an organization. It would often be referred to colloquially as 'the way we do things round here'. Some organizational cultures rely heavily on the written word, on careful statements about what top managers are in business to achieve. In other organizational cultures such precision would be seen as the ropes tying down Gulliver. In some organizations there will be very rigid rules indeed about, for example, authority over capital expenditure or the right to dismiss an employee or the right (very important in the context of this book) to appoint someone to a managerial job.

Aneurin Bevan gave in his largely autobiographical political treatise *In Place of Fear* an evocative statement about the pursuit of power which I have never seen equalled in a management book, though its themes apply equally to management. He describes how he pursued power through his involvement first in the most junior levels of politics in a village in Wales and then through ascending series of political involvements until he reached the House of Commons and finally the Cabinet. Before each political level he thought *that* was where real power lay – only to find each time that there was yet another level beyond. Although many of them have gone through similar processes, middle and senior managers do not recognize how constrained the jobs of the people at the top often are, viewing them as the major power positions in the organization where the constraints of having someone over you finally disappear. While the board is the most powerful position in an organization (and putting aside issues of responsibilities to shareholders), organizational culture, and organizational structure which is a partial aspect of it, inhibit as much as they assist the ways in which board members work. 'The way we do things round here' may be expressed directly and immediately by the way in which a top manager carries out his job, but that has been influenced by the way things have been round here probably for quite a long time.

Cultural values

In recent years a number of books have attempted to describe company cultures. The difference in intention between them and books about individual management processes is not wholly clear, not least because it is only the individual effort of individual managers which actually registers finally the totality of the company culture. From the point of view of developing effective managers, there is a certain paradox in the popularity of *In Search of Excellence*.[1] Although it says that 'excellent' companies tend to spend more time and trouble over management development and training than less excellent companies, the book is remarkably deficient in any suggestions on how a company might change its managers and develop them in order to become an excellent company. What it does have however is a well-connected series of analyses and vivid pen pictures describing both individuals and, more importantly for this section, the total culture of some excellent companies.

If we put aside the fascinating claim of cause and effect, not established to the satisfaction of all readers, we are still left with the undoubted fact that excellent or not and permanently excellent or not the authors do describe organizations in which there are very strong cultural requirements affecting how their managers behave. Their research established that their excellent companies have values that are clear, acted on and well understood deep in the ranks. While it could be argued that some other than excellent companies might have values of much the same intensity, they certainly identify some crucial aspects of organizational culture. Family feelings, service, innovation, a rich pattern of legends and parables exist in their excellent companies and perhaps more widely. The IBM slogan 'IBM means service' is important because it is carried out in practice; the organization lives and means it. This could be compared with an organizational culture where they found 325 task forces not one of which had finished in the previous three years, nor had any been disbanded. Here the cultural phenomenon which presumably influenced the managers was that they should look as if they were doing something rather than actually achieving anything.

Peters and Waterman say that virtually all their excellent companies had a well-defined set of beliefs. Less well-performing institutions were marked by one of two characteristics; many had no set of coherent beliefs at all while others had distinctive objectives but the only ones that really meant anything were the ones that could be quantified in terms of finance, such as earnings per share and gross measures. The distinction between these three different positions is important for their argument but not for our understanding in this book. Cultural beliefs about the value of specific financial targets alone may be insufficient to produce excellent companies, but they certainly influence managers so long as the companies survive. ITT under Geneen, at which we shall be looking on page 159, had very clear values although 'only' dominated by 'the bottom line'. Indeed the authors go on to say 'companies with overriding financial objectives may do a pretty good job of motivating the top 15 or even 50. But these objectives seldom add much zest to life down the line.'

Some illustrations of culture

Interestingly they say that values are not usually transmitted through formal written procedures but through stories, myths, legends and metaphors. As we shall see later, these are particularly transmitted through and about the owner, originator or chief executive of the business. Their research is in line with the reality I have experienced. It is most obviously true in family businesses where the example of the Watsons in IBM can be repeated elsewhere. I worked once in an industry not well known for its humanitarian attitude to its employees or for its dedication to giving value for money. The cultural belief of my particular organization however had been established many years before by a chief executive who insisted that the customer should not be given work which although meeting the specification was of poor quality. Similarly his attitude to his employees was by the standards of his day one of enlightened paternalism in a dismal industry.

Of the eight organizations in which I have been employed, five had distinctive and recognisable ways of carrying out the management tasks. Each had strong cultural characteristics, though culture was only one of several variables which also included the nature of the industry and the particular economic environment in which they were operating. Here are two of the companies concerned, with the characteristics predominant at a particular time on the main board.

Company A

Run on 'high wall' separate functional lines
Barons running the functions retained power by denying co-operation to others
All experienced over many years in the industry and largely within the same firm
All had only narrow functional experience on their way to the top.
Dominated by design, production and sales, not marketing.
General management occurred only through the chief executive.

Had an incoherent mixture of centralization and decentralization

Had recently experienced near-disaster

Company B

General management (the control of real profit centres) existed at least at three levels.

Half the board had significant though more junior experience in management outside the firm and the industry.

The directors' experience was limited either functionally or geographically.

The company operated on an explicit organizational value and structure of decentralization.

It had a four-year period of significant success.

Different though these two organizations were in many respects, one shared feature was that both gave explicit attention to management development, but the effective operation was largely confined to junior and middle management. Another shared phenomenon was that neither board was required to operate as a team in the sense of developing and sharing corporate responsibilities for decisions in areas of the individual directors' work. One exception in company B was in the area of top management development, where a consensus was operated for decisions about managerial appointments which was quite at variance with the requirement that directors should take independent decisions or other issues.

In both organizations there was a strong requirement for formal corporate plans, which like many others were long on analysis and hope and short on competitor understanding and implementation. In both cases there was very substantial involvement of top management, and in both cases naturally the corporate plan showed how the company was to move into an era of great success. There were in fact weaknesses both in the nature of the plans and in the ability of the directors concerned to implement them. The organizational requirement for the production of immensely detailed plans changed under the impact of declining performance. Directors were now promoted (or acquired) who were capable of taking the drains up, appearing for management meetings at 7.30 am, and cutting head count savagely. Top managers previously decried as lacking vision, strategic sense and the ability to take people with them suddenly became more valued in a culture which needed to adapt to the more brutal reality of the present. As this example shows, culture itself is affected by a number of circumstances.

Organization structure

Organization structure itself will determine in part what managers do. If as with company B a number of separate profit centres are established, the organizations will at least talk about, and conceivably will act upon, the need to develop general managers to run the profit centres. If the structure of the organization from the smallest units right through to the main board is strictly functional, so that managers proceed up narrow lines of finance or sales or production, the organization is unlikely, unless it takes the kind of explicit action spelled out in earlier chapters, to produce managers capable of running profit centres well. If the organization is based on product, or industry served, or geography, then again what managers at the top will be required to do is to manage those separate activities successfully. If the structure is mainly geared to handling the problems of markets, the directors concerned will manage themselves and be assessed against the criteria of how well the needs of the markets are being met. If the business is organized to manufacture products or to service people the same comments apply. The weight of priorities felt through the structure will help to determine what managers do and therefore what development processes are likely to fit them to do it.

It is of course the discovery that highly separate organization lines with powerful independent non-communicating baronies do not necessarily produce an effective organizational result that brings about the demand for more complicated structures. This may be a formal matrix or may be all sorts of informal processes of joint working parties, co-ordinators, attempting to draw together separate processes for the common good. When any of these changes is introduced the organization will find that it lacks the managers in every area, but not least at the top, capable of managing the new process successfully.

In the previous organization structure supported by the old-style culture, managers were encouraged and enabled to pursue independent goals. Now they are suddenly required to reveal to colleagues problems which they had spent years hiding, to share resources instead of holding on to their own. The design director is now to be obliged to treat his manufacturing director as a colleague instead of as an enemy. All these examples indicate how the behavioural requirements and therefore development needs may change.

The issues of structure and culture are well described by Charles Handy.[2] The culture he describes as 'role culture' was in his view the one which classical management theorists thought they were describing – the management of the steady state. He believes that in many modern organizations the 'task culture' describes both the appropriate organizational form and the kind of behaviour which managers will need to exhibit.

Figure 9.2 shows changes in the culture of one organization over a period of time.

New cultural values	*Old cultural values*
profit centres	budget centres
results orientation	activities orientation
organizational conflict	organizational neatness
immediate	important
customer satisfaction	getting a sale
confrontation	concealment
open personal relationships	closed personal relationships
long hours	official hours
lateral thinking	normal thinking
solution centred	problem dominated
trade-offs	we can't

Figure 9.2 New cultural values and old cultural values

Management research over the last 25 years has shown how necessary it is to see organization structure and managerial tasks as being contingent upon a wide range of factors. There are no clear and universally appropriate messages on either structure or managerial behaviour. The process for example of shared decision-making, as compared with the relatively autocratic style of some managers, can be shown to be effective in some circumstances and ineffective in others. While therefore it is superficially attractive to talk about 'good' managers and 'bad' managers, once we get below the surface it seems that attributes seen as bad in some cultures are seen as good in others. Trying to match the requirements for effective performance by a manager with the objective requirements of the business and its culture will tend to produce managers who are 'good' at least in the context of that culture and that organization.

Those objective requirements may change under the impact of the variety of factors mentioned in this chapter. Further, it could be argued that in some organizations the nature of the culture may inhibit effective performance, because the culture defines processes and behaviour which do not lead to the optimum managerial performance. The development processes experienced by managers on their way to the top may therefore be appropriate to needs perceived at the time, but inappropriate to needs recognized by the time they reach the top, or to needs which may be recognized later.

One answer is to try to introduce changes in development and training processes at the managerial level to meet changes in behaviour recognized as desirable in the organization's future culture. This is very difficult because it presumes someone can guess what the future culture will be. Indeed the reference made to participative as compared with autocratic management processes shows us how attempts to change managerial behaviour within an existing context can be unproductive. Personnel or training and development specialists have sometimes sponsored and introduced development processes, guiding managers towards a participative style. Such training is a waste of time if it is too far out of key with what the organization's current culture will actually reward. At the worst it produces confusion and dissatisfaction amongst the managers concerned.

Experience of work under the heading of 'Organization Development' seems clearly to show that attempts to change the cultural style of management by working from the bottom upwards is ineffective. The fact that any desired change in the culture ought therefore to be designed and implemented from the top is another factor which should cause directors to recognize that they may themselves need to undertake learning and development processes in order to redefine the organizational culture and make it more appropriate to current needs.

The influence of the chairman or chief executive

One of the more interesting aspects of the Peters and Waterman book was their identification of the fact that the climate and culture of many of the organizations they studied had been set originally by a single powerful figure, often the person who had set up the business. This is of course more likely to be recognizable when the business is relatively modern, as in the case of Hewlett Packard or IBM. We know however that the powerful figure at the top can influence the style of management processes in his organization in businesses of much longer standing. (Although there are many fewer women chief executives in our survey, the small amount of evidence about them suggests that they will have a similar impact.)

It would of course seem entirely logical that the top person in the organization should have a significant influence on what other managers do. The way in which they influence seems rarely to be through detailed job descriptions, allocation of priorities or discussion of objectives. There are however a number of other signals to top managers on what they should do.

Explicit and implicit signals

The signals may sometimes be very explicit. Chief executives set the agenda – both the what and the how – for any discussion which occurs, formally for formal meetings or by actually determining what is discussed at the many informal meetings they will have. For outside meetings their concerns will be revealed by the internal memoranda they write, the questions they ask as they go round the business, the telephone calls they make, the total impact of things which they show to be important.

They demonstrate their lack of concern for other issues by not writing about them, by never asking questions, by cutting short discussion. I have seen a chief executive go through the motions of a meeting to discuss an apparently important topic but demonstrate by reading other papers, by taking telephone calls or even by leaving the room that in fact he had no real interest in the subject under discussion. These are implicit signals, without the directness of the written word.

Sometimes explicit and implicit signals about what is seen to be important are in conflict. In our survey we found illustrations of how these signals work on the issue of management development. In one organization the explicit signals were clear because the organization had a written policy, set targets for the amount of management training to be undertaking, and a variety of internal messages indicating that the chief executive took the subject seriously. This was accompanied by an implicit signal, because the chief executive had attended, for a discussion session, 43 out of 46 courses run for top managers in his organization over the previous 10 years. In addition to the benefits for himself, the implicit signal given clearly was in tune with the explicit signal about management development.

In another organization the explicit signal about management development was that it was important: the chief executive signed each year a memorandum defining and setting up the management development process. Certain aspects of the process were stated to be obligatory. However, the explicit message of seriousness was contradicted by the implicit message conveyed by the fact that the chief executive gave no further significant sign of interest in the process after the despatch of the memorandum.

An organization in which I worked was moving into formal corporate planning at the time when this was very much in vogue. The chief executive concerned marked the draft corporate plan 'filed unread'. This fact became known in the organization, with consequences for the seriousness with which his colleagues and lower level managers took the corporate planning process.

A chief executive in a different organization set great store by reviewing performance through presentations made by the responsible managers, including main board directors. He showed how important he regarded this particular role of his top people by allocating time and asking challenging questions on the occasion. In the early days he also required a rehearsal of the presentation. At one such rehearsal he stopped the presentation and told the main board director concerned to return on the following day, a Saturday

morning, with a more effective one. Here the chief executive rein-
forced his explicit and implicit signals about both the style of presentation and, even more importantly, the content.

The biographies of great managerial figures, the most powerful
actors in the drama of management, similarly indicate how explicit
and implicit signals are offered. In the case of Geneen of ITT the
explicit signal was that his directors were to be concerned about
'the bottom line', and certainty about the bottom line was to be
ensured through an organizational structure emphasizing a network of checks and balances, the use of large structured meetings as
the focus for monitoiing and improving performance, and the
encouragement of conflict as the process for bringing out what he
called 'unshakable facts'. Top managers in ITT either responded
satisfactorily to the style Geneen set or they left the organization or
disappeared into a position out of sight.

While the biographies of Iacocca and Michael Edwardes may in
some respects over-emphasize the weight of their personal contribution, other evidence about BL and Chrysler supports the view
that very often a powerful and dominant leader at the top will
largely determine the nature of what his immediate subordinates
on the board will do, or he will replace them with others who will
follow his agenda.

Not all chief executives will operate in the same dramatic highly
personalized style. Some organizations for at least part of their history successfully operate without a dominant chief executive;
others operate unsuccessfully with a dominant chief executive.
Naturally enough where there is no dominant top man there may be
strong personalities on the board who will determine for themselves
what they will do and how they will do it. The ambiguity of the concept of leadership, the difficulty of defining it in operational terms,
is illustrated by the different styles adopted by successful chief
executives.

The forceful, dominant, aggressive style is one which would normally be easily characterized as 'leadership'. A chief executive who
operates in a less visible and forceful style would be superficially
characterized as less of a 'leader' but might be equally effective in
some circumstances. The circumstances may change, as seems to
be the case in the shift from a relatively collective board decision-
making process in ICI to one in which John Harvey-Jones as chairman both clarified board responsibilities and inserted a more

visible role for himself. How far what he decided to do was a function of this own style and successful experience, and how far it was
an objective result of circumstances, is not at all clear. What is clear
is that he certainly took a frontal position in changing a good many
of the existing characteristics of the ICI culture, and of the expectations about what he and other board directors would be doing.

Organizational objectives

In logic and in textbook philosophy what top managers do ought to
be determined first by the objectives of the organization. As in so
many other respects organizational life does not work that way,
which is why this issue appears third in this discussion of influences
on what top managers do. Objectives are not normally set out on a
blank piece of paper unaffected either by past history or by the
views of the powerful figures currently running the organization.
The process of determining objectives may be more influential on
what managers do than the actual content of the objectives.

As in many other areas of managerial life, the difference between
espoused purposes and beliefs and actual behaviour may be considerable. However, the objective set for an organization has at
least some influence. The seminal article by Theodore Levitt[3]
which raised the question 'What business are we in?' has seeped
into the consciousness of many directors even where they have
neither read the article nor been on a course derived from it.

While the responses to the question in different organizations
have been diverse, not to say peculiar or irrational, most boards
would now recognize that one of their main functions is to establish
a view of what the business is trying to achieve. The view may range
from a relatively simple-minded approach to doing anything which
will create a profit to a mixture of different objectives, which may
for example try to combine high levels of profit with a high reputation for service and a concern for the needs of the local community.
The messages about these objectives may be explicit – agreed and
circulated in writing – or implicit. There may be confusion, compounded at times of organizational stress or change, about how
significant particular objectives are. Concern for the employee as a
person may be easier to sustain at times of high profitability than at
times of financial disaster.

The activities of top managers may therefore be influenced to a greater or lesser extent by the objectives of the organization as stated or understood. If the organization is essentially concerned to continue on successful paths, it will give emphasis to activities and functions believed to have contributed to that success. An organization whose success is attributed to high quality production processes will give emphasis to discussion and then implementation of these processes at the top level. If marketing is seen as the significant process, that will secure air time. In these cases, as we have shown in earlier chapters, the paths to the top will be similarly influenced by what are preceived to be the central activities in the organization.

If, however, the organization sets itself a different target, of development and growth outside its current success, top management attention and effort will switch to other activities and processes. In these circumstances, the requirement that top managers should be able to undertake the writing of corporate strategy and the determination of a corporate plan becomes more significant. If these strategies and plans depend upon acquisition or divestment, either an existing board member has to be given the opportunity to manage them, or a new board member may be brought on.

The acquisition of other organizations may bring in quite different cultures and personalities and styles of management significantly dissimilar from those of the acquiring organization. The requirements for effective management of a steady state organization may be supplanted by those for managing an organization in turbulence.

A director may then be faced with the need to manage activities of which he has no previous experience, run by managers more knowledgeable in that business. They may be demonstrably effective in it, and also have clear ideas about how they secured their success. A stable structured business used to managing by careful analysis may find itself with a cuckoo in the nest whose processes are much more quickly responsive to perhaps different needs, and whose managers behave in quite different ways.

Directors in the new structure may therefore face conflict between their previously successful way of doing business with subordinates and what their new subordinates may see as desirable. In contrast with the previous sections the situation may be one in which the powerful influence of the chief executive is less significant than the influence of powerful subordinates.

Directorial imperatives

If the board does not direct the future of the business, the direction of the business will be determined by managers below the board. Even strategic direction may be undertaken more or less successfully lower down. Indeed this seems to be true for any specific board resonsibility. Maximum effectiveness however is usually attainable only if objectives are decided at the top (whatever the contribution from below); if the nature of the business and its boundaries are set there: and if the processes of achieving what it is desired to achieve are directed and monitored from the top. Effective managers lower down will sometimes fill a vacuum. The choice as to whether the board gives directions must be made by explicit decision rather than implicit abnegation.

One important area in which a board should be directly involved is that of developing people for the top jobs – its own successors. Sometimes however there is a conflict with the facts of the organization structure. It is easier to control the development of managers from the top in a centralized structure. In a decentralized one managers lower down may feel that interference from the top is in conflict with their responsibility to manage their independent profit centres.

As we found in our survey, decentralization can make it impossible for the main board to ensure an appropriate succession for themselves. When this defect becomes apparent, the board may have to introduce some element of monitoring and control on executive development even where this is in conflict with other aspects of organizational beliefs. There are decisions which only the board can take, because in the absence of board level activity the business may not survive.

This is illustrated again when a business needs to adapt to new circumstances or to take advantage of them. The direction and purposes of the organization may need to change. Yet change is natural only in the sense that it is a frequent occurrence; it is not natural in the sense that effective and economic change is easily secured.

An organization's employees, not least people at the top, may understand the economic requirement for change, but the processes by which this is to be achieved are usually less clear to them. Again, there can be little doubt that change is most effectively led from the top; lower down the organization, the climate of performance and rewards for it is nearly always geared to the shorter term, except in research departments. Concern for the longer term is one of the normal functions of a board. Without definition and push from the top, the implementation of change is unlikely to be a high priority lower down.

Change is a general and not a functional issue; it cannot be allocated to any particular department such as research or product development. Change can indeed embrace everything an organization is attempting to do and how it achieves it. When a board recognizes the need to grasp this role for itself, it then begins to think about the processes it needs to set up as well as the particular objectives it wishes to secure.

Kanter[4] has given by far the most persuasive and wide-reaching view of what this involves. Her research shows that organizations successful in achieving innovations are those which encourage creativity through large-scale processes of integration. They design structures, implement participative management processes and encourage teamwork in pursuit of success on innovative projects. Organizations less effective in encouraging innovation operate segments with little real communication on substantive issues, in which individual performers for the most part are indifferent to the efforts and achievements of the units. In these cases she is of course defining the kind of organization structure and culture which has not recognized that such processes will not produce change, often no doubt because they do not value the processes or results of change.

Where change is defined as desirable, then the range of activities necessary to accomplish it makes a push from the top imperative. If Kanter is right in saying an integrative structure and culture is the first requirement, then individual efforts at change lower down are by definition likely to be flawed and at least less successful than they need to be. Equally the board itself must demonstrate the integrative structure and culture in its own activities if change is to be fully effective.

In discussing these two particular cases of directorial decision making on important issues I hope to have made a general point about what top managers do. Some at least do not what is obvious, not what is personally pleasant and rewarding, not solely what past and present culture and organizational structure reward them for doing. They are concerned with issues vital for the success of the organization, which may bring them into conflict with other aspects of their work.

Technology, or the processes of the organization

The double description is necessary because technology would by many be assumed to describe the processes used in manufacturing industry. We are concerned here with the requirements placed on top managers by the processes employed to carry out the work of the organization. For example, a large oil company may cover the processes of discovering, bringing out, carrying, storing and delivering oil. Any of these technologies is different from that of a service industry such as banking or hotels, where the process of producing and delivering is substantially different. Some technologies, such as shipbuilding or motorway construction, emphasize the routine and easily definable processes, subject to constant repetition. They are well proven and contain relatively few possibilities for error within the technology itself. Other technologies are either inherently subject to more possibilities of risk, or are at a stage of development where the possibility of error or indeed of new opportunities is still being discovered. These of course are only a few illustrations of the wide variety of technology and service, which demands different kinds of managerial work. Defining and managing the work of people operating at the frontiers of knowledge requires a different sort of attention to relationships, for example, from managing the work of people whose concern is not how but how much.

Size

There seems to be no clear correlation between size and what top managers do, not least because organizations of much the same size choose different organization structures, have different cultures and operate in different technologies. It is possible to find large organizations with a multi-layered rule-bound bureaucracy, it is also possible to find small organizations with a great deal of what they would describe as systems, order and procedure rather than bureaucracy. Three large multinational organizations I looked at in

1982, for example, had head offices employing variously 1800, 150 and 25. The size of a diversified decentralized conglomerate has much less influence on what managers do than the fact that it *is* decentralized and diversified.

Rewards

In Chapter 1 we considered the results from our survey on questions about psychological and financial rewards for development, and Chapter 11 draws out some of the theoretical issues involved in the expectations about the consequences of development. The expectation of rewards of different kinds (and perhaps punishments also) must have a big influence on what managers do over the full range of their activities.

The question of what, in terms of expected rewards, influences individuals is one which leads to easy and misleading generalizations. 'People at the top are driven by a strong achievement motivation.' 'Unless tax rates are lowered, the willingness to take risks will disappear.' Such generalizations are quite laughable to anyone who has experienced the complex range of influences reviewed in this chapter and the previous one. How influential are tax rates in organizational cultures which reject new ideas?

The matrix of influences derived from different kinds of reward is complex, and that complexity is compounded by the response of particular individuals to that matrix. Contingency rules again! Perhaps the most useful comment in the development context is that whereas many directorial activities are expected to emphasize the long term, rewards are often either geared to or experienced as short term. The fact that directors are judged on the basis of short-term results, not long-term plans, 'when the chips are down' is an expression of this.

Summary

The skills directors need are defined by the particulars of the job they do. What they do is determined initially by the objective requirements of the job, but these in turn are influenced by what is happening around the job and by expectations created by the culture and structure of the organization. What directors do is particularly affected by the personal behaviour of the chief executive. The commitment of the chief executive and his colleagues to sustaining or changing the purpose, direction and processes of the organization may cause changes in the requirements for effective performance.

The specifics of particular directorial jobs, influenced by all these factors, produce both a requirement for personal development and an interest in it.

References

1   Peters, T. and Waterman, R.H., *In Search of Excellence*, Harper & Row, New York, 1983
2   Handy, C., *Understanding Organisations*, Penguin Books, London, 1985
3   Levitt, T., 'Marketing myopia', *Harvard Business Review*, July/Aug. 1960
4   Kanter, R.M., *The Change Masters*, Simon & Schuster, New York, 1983

10 Other influences on managers

Let us turn now to the external environment. As I have watched and listened to managers over the last 20 years, I have become more and more conscious of the validity of the saying 'Success has many fathers, failure has none'. One of the failures in many performance appraisal schemes is that they insufficiently discuss how far any individual's performance is affected by circumstances outside his or her control, favourable and unfavourable. It is also understandable that managers are more frequently inclined to attribute success to the contribution they have personally made and to discount the influence of factors outside themselves. Conversely, when things go wrong they are more inclined to recognize the impact of the external environment and in colourful and persuasive detail the impact of the fall in value of the dollar, a change in government policy or yet another shift in oil production and prices. As some of the participants in our survey told us, in a slightly different context about career progress, it is important not to be in the wrong place at the wrong time.

One of the distinguishing characteristics of the influences affecting managerial work from outside the organization is that most of those discussed below are not personal and do not express themselves strongly through individual managerial behaviour. Whereas organization structure, culture, objectives and imperatives in different ways are statements about what one person requires of another in the organization, many of those mentioned below are relatively impersonal factors.

Characteristics of the industry or service

In addition to the technological differences discussed in the previous chapter, industries can be defined by their position on the economic graph. They may be in a position of growth, turbulence or decline which will have a direct effect on the possibilities of achievement. Managers will be pushed into activities more appropriate to growth (exploitation of revenue possibilities) or decline (cost reduction). A growth strategy will lead to a greater variety of responsibilities and roles and in the modern world, for example, might well include more international activity. As with the individual organization but on a larger scale, growth industries may contain a bigger requirement for risk taking management, whereas an industry in decline offers fewer opportunities but is inherently more stable and controllable.

Competition

Competition can occur in industries of any characteristics whether growing, declining, standing still or merely turbulent. I know of organizations which had no experience at the top level of managing against competition. When they undertook a strategy which launched them into countries where they have not operated before they were unable to forecast the competitive reaction, and subsequently unable to manage the consequences of it.

In another organization many of the top directors had experience of sharp competition, particularly in the United States. This experience enabled them to recognize the reality of competition worldwide and influenced their capacity to deal with it. This is not the place for a basic economic lecture on capitalism and how competition is alternately encouraged and discouraged by the capitalist process. The point here is simply that the presence or absence of sharp competition will significantly affect the priorities adopted for the business. Competition may well, for example, encourage people at the top to follow the organizational imperative of change, pursuing innovation rather than simply improvement.

Politics

Directors are constantly saddened, surprised and sometimes disgusted to find that politicians make decisions for political reasons. Where these decisions are either directly about the goods or services which an organization provides, or provide the economic background to them, businessmen faced with disadvantageous consequences blame the process rather than the decision. Politicians reaching a decision seen as illogical by a businessman must clearly have made the decision by an illogical process called Political Thinking. One of my least successful efforts when I was a management trainer was to get an articulate and moderate politician to explain to a group of managers the relationship between politics and industry. Ironically they understood much more easily the explanation of a trade unionist about his relationship to management. People from industry and commerce do not recognize in themselves the same kind of double standards which they believe to exist in politicians. It is not unknown for the same industrialist to ask for both less intervention in general by the government and more intervention on a particular issue of specific concern to him.

The consequences of political decisions may be of many different kinds. A political organization such as a council or indeed a government may refuse to trade with a particular organization because of distaste for its relationship with South Africa or with its employees or ex-employees. It may set general rules of conduct affecting managerial processes, for example requiring commitment to Equal Opportunities regardless of race or sex. At the highest level political decisions can determine ownership or the nature of competition. Privatization, for example of British Telecom, produced different demands on managers.

The issue of competition has been sharpened in the United Kingdom and the United States by governmental acts requiring deregulation, affecting both the general business performance and the specific managerial task of airlines and banks. With airlines it seems that while the impact on competition and business was severe the impact on managerial activities was less formidable. In the case of A T & T, which was required to split up into separate companies, the managerial requirements in the newly created profit centres were substantially different from those which applied previously.

Ownership

The public or private ownership issue is not of course the only ownership issue. Businesses family owned or owned by anonymous shareholders may cause directors to behave in quite different ways to meet different priorities and time scales.

Non-executive directors

The one directly personal influence comparable to those mentioned under the internal environment (Chapter 9) is that of the non-executive colleagues of directors. If we put aside the purely cosmetic reasons for their presence, and look rather at their real potential contribution, we see that they may influence their colleagues by some of the means mentioned earlier, particularly the determination of objectives and the choice of issues on which the board determines to take action. They may be influential here precisely because they often bring a different kind of knowledge, experience and contact to the board. Where they are satisfied with neither the strategy nor the implementation of it, non-executive directors, possibly through their non-executive chairman, are apparently increasingly prepared to dispose of the chief executive and perhaps some of his colleagues. Awareness of this power might influence the performance of directors by causing them to do things to satisfy the non-executive directors. This may of course be a bad thing as much as a good.

We were surprised to find in our survey, in which we talked only to executive directors, how little comment was made about the influence of external directors, though it is true we were asking about learning and development processes rather than the total performance of the job. It seemed that their influence was scarcely noticeable. This may have attributed either to the extraordinary subtlety with which they exercise that influence, or to a failure actually to exercise any.

National cultures

A common language has no doubt helped to contribute to the use of American management literature in the United Kingdom. As anyone who has even visited the United States, let alone worked there, will confirm, there are nevertheless significant differences between the cultures at a management level as at many others.

Managers from the United Kingdom with responsibilities for the United States, or vice versa, have found from bitter experience that even within the same organization the requirements for effective managerial performance sometimes differ substantially. Sometimes what look like national differences turn out to be more related to different kinds of business or different cultures in organizational terms in one country as compared with another. A number of the differences are however national in origin, of which one would be the relative openness of style of many American managers as compared with the relative reserve of many British managers. American managers may in the middle and late 1980s be less shocked by the attitudes of British managers to trade unions than they were before 1979. They will still find that British managers are more likely to expect warmth in personal relationships to be earned rather than immediately offered as in America.

American colleagues, either as chief executives or as peers on the board, are therefore likely to challenge the attitudes and specific behaviour of British colleagues. Not only is the actual challenge often difficult for directors to cope with but the method of expression may compound the difficulty. It may be bad enough to have your experience and ideas challenged but, as I observed it in one organization, it is even more difficult to accept that the challenge is offered directly rather than by implication, and is accompanied by a clear value judgement that challenge is an inherently desirable process and nothing to do with personal likes or dislikes. It is quite contrary to the cultural British norms that a manager who perceives himself as on friendly terms with an American should be confronted with extremely damaging evidence at a meeting.

There are now an increasing number of studies showing how

necessary it is to add the cultural dimension to all those we have discussed so far in looking at influences on what managers actually do. When variables such as the nature of the job, the type of organization and even organizational culture have been eliminated or allowed for, a residue of differences is left which can only be explained by reference to the national culture.

The most important author in this field, Hofstede,[1] defined culture as 'a collective programming of the mind'. It derives from basic values, for example freedom as compared with equality, which in turn leads to role expectations and to particular behaviour. Cultural issues arise from basic factors such as gross inequalities in autocratic countries such as many in Latin America as compared with democratic countries with a much smaller range of income such as the United Kingdom and Germany. Hofstede has shown that cultural differences substantially affect styles of management as revealed by measurements on an Authoritarian as compared with a Participative scale, and by the openness or secretiveness of communication.

Through business contacts and books about Japan we are now much more aware than we used to be that Western culture emphasizes the individual and oriental culture the group. In the Far East decision-making is more likely to be seen as the prerogative of the man at the top, and sharing it (as distinct from contributing to it) is much more difficult. Promotion may be seen as much more to do with personal status than with increased responsibility. The idea of women in management may be even more bizarre to many countries outside the UK and the United States than it is within them.

Cultural differences express themselves as differences in the way managers both behave themselves and expect others to behave. While on first acquaintance ignorance about the cultural norms of others may lead to incorrect expectations, over a period of time expectations may create stereotypes. Hofstede quotes a case study run at a business school, the data from which were analysed by country. The French pushed up the problem to their superiors, the Germans would have resolved it by setting up some rules, and the British by discussion and by improving communications. Stereotyped expectations however can sometimes be misleading. In an organization involving British and German managers, in which I acted as consultant, complaints were made about undue attention to the organization structure, a bureaucratic wish to communicate everything in writing and a constant reference to rules. It was however the Germans who were complaining about the British!

An interesting example of how different cultures influence a manager's behaviour is given by Doktor.[2] As we saw in the previous chapter, the characteristic picture identified by researchers from America and Britain was of managers who engaged in very short interactions. In Doktor's research on American and Japanese top managers there was substantial similarity in the amount of time the chief executives spent alone; there was a substantial dissimilarity in the length of time spent on particular activities. Whereas half of American executive activities were completed in nine minutes or less only 18 per cent of the Japanese activities were completed in this time. It is not possible without further analysis to say which of the two groups is more effective in meeting which managerial objectives. While it might be that the Japanese executives are more successful in sustaining good interpersonal relationships, perhaps the Americans get more things done in a given period of time.

The whole person

These last two chapters have described how factors outside the individual influence what he or she does in a top management role. These factors are encouraged or contradicted by the personality and psychological make-up of the individual involved.

Attempts by psychologists to describe these factors are sometimes expressed in language wholly incomprehensible to the ordinary manager, or alternatively in superficially understandable language which is in fact misleading. A more fundamental problem in the context of this book is that the behaviour which may emerge as a result of a manager's individual personality is observable and perhaps capable of being changed. Internal drives such as 'motivation', the most favoured of all, are by definition not directly observable, but are deduced from some observable behaviour.

It seems probable that psychological make-up is not only difficult to identify because it is deeply embedded, but difficult to influence for the same reason. Psychoanalysts and psychotherapists take a long time to help patients achieve even an understanding of their personalities, let alone influence the expression of them. Since this book is concerned with effective action, and understanding the organizational and managerial background within which it can be taken, I have chosen to put the issue of personality to one side.

There are however some facts about the whole person which are worth identifying. First, managers and directors exist outside the office; they have a home life, sometimes shared at varying levels of intensity with husbands, wives, other kinds of partner and children. Geneen wanted his executives to be available for him to call at any time on any day of the week. Iacocca says that he protects his weekends, although he works fiercely during the week. Iacocca implied that he made this choice before he became chief executive. Some managers make similar choices, with implications about at least when they do their job and to some extent how they do it.

In earlier chapters we have discussed some of the issues concerning the development of women for top jobs. For the purpose of this chapter it is important to identify whether women as a group do their job differently from men as a group. The evidence on this is not entirely clear. An article by Susan Fraker[3] claims that a matched study of 2000 managers showed women do not manage differently from men. But Marshall[4] shows that women managers are more likely to seek interdependence than independence and possess qualities such as co-operation, tolerance and ready adjustment to change to a greater degree than men. Marshall moves on to consider whether women should be pushed into behaving like the male stereotype of a 'good' manager, and Simmons[5] asks whether the reverse is applicable: why should not male managers be encouraged to develop those attributes more normally seen as feminine?

Some potential influences arising from the type of person who becomes top manager have not yet significantly emerged in practice. I have no evidence as to whether heterosexual domination at top level has been changed and if so how this might influence the performance of either lesbians or gays in managerial roles. Even in the late 1980s it may be that cultural norms inhibit managers from 'coming out of the closet'.

The other minority groups are not able to conceal themselves in a similar way and therefore their absence is visible. Ethnic minorities have not reached the boards of most UK companies, so we have no knowledge as to whether their ethnic properties would influence their performance as top managers, although we might guess from the cultural information available that they would indeed do so.

Evidence from the United States seems to be more concerned with blacks running their own businesses, such as the owner of Ebony. Changes in opportunities at the political level have occurred in the United Kingdom over recent years, at first in local government but, after the 1987 General Election, in Parliament also, with four non-white MPs.

The range of influences

Is the director's job influenced by a wider range of factors than those of managers lower down? In some organizations this is probably true. It is however more accurate to say that some influences, especially those of ownership and politics, are experienced more intensively at the top. The range of influences outlined at the beginning of the previous chapter is shown in more detail in Figure 10.1, which may serve as a summary of these two chapters.

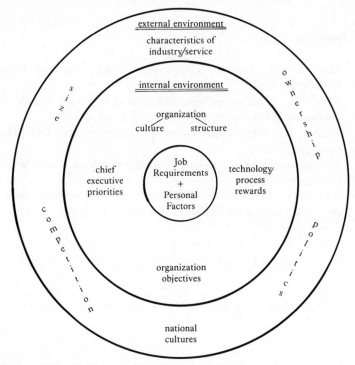

Figure 10.1 Influences on directors' jobs

Implications for Development

The factors discussed in this chapter influence development in two ways – content and process. They influence *content* because they help to shape the events to which directors respond, and thereby create demands for effective managerial behaviour. They influence *process* because they help to establish the context within which development is sponsored, encouraged and rewarded.

It would be much more convenient if we could treat development as a process about which generalizations could be made. Indeed that has so far been the principle followed by manys schemes and courses. If we want to make development real, and responsive to differing situations, the complexities revealed through this chapter are unavoidable. Since the job actually done is the core of development, we must understand the job in order to manage development.

References

1   Hofstede, G., *Culture's Consequences*, Sage, Beverley Hills, California, 1980
2   Doktor, R., 'Culture and the Management of Time', *Asia Pacific Journal of Management*, vol. no. 1, 1983, pp. 65–71
3   Fraker, S., 'Why Women Aren't Getting to the Top', *Fortune*, 16.4.84
4   Marshall, J., *Women Managers: Travellers in a Male World*, Wiley, Chichester, 1984
5   Simmons, M., 'Undoing Men's Gender Conditioning', *Industrial and Commercial Training*, Nov./Dec. 1986, pp. 21–4

11 Learning and development: influences

Up to this point we have described the various ways in which managers have learned on their way to the top. We have looked at actual experiences and at the opportunities which can be categorized by those experiences.

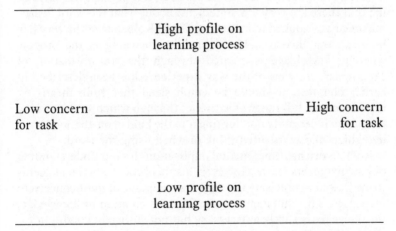

Training and education courses normally have a high profile for learning, low for task. Responsibility for applications is left with the learner.

On-the-job management has high concern for task, low for learning. Getting the result is what matters; learning is a low priority.

Figure 11.1 Task and learning – perceptions

Although it is possible to identify a wide range of learning opportunities, few managers seem to take advantage of the full range. Perhaps this is because the opportunity was lacking, or was not recognized, or they preferred not to take it. Part of the reason is the imbalance in perception of learning within the task – a problem which training and education attempt to resolve (Figure 11.1).

In this chapter we shall try to help managers understand better what learning and development involve, and to show how they can improve their ability both to assess what they need to learn and improve their capacity to do so.

What is learning?

Since remarkably little attention has been paid to the nature of learning in those institutions such as business schools in which learning is supposedly the prime purpose, it is perhaps not surprising that there are very few statements about what the word 'learning' means as applied to managers. David Kolb, one of the very few high-ranking theorists, has defined it; 'learning is the process whereby knowledge is created through the transformation of experience'.[1] In view of the way experience has been described in earlier chapters, it should be emphasized that Kolb means by experience the full range of activities through which someone may learn, and is certainly not limiting it to the kind of on-the-job learning which managers often think of when using the word.

Kolb's work has fundamental implications for our understanding of how managers learn. However, his theoretical statement seems to me flawed in precisely the area that would be of most concern to managers. The statement emphasizes the creation of knowledge; this however is surely a necessary but not sufficient condition for the process of learning. It is precisely because formal learning processes have so often emphasized the acquisition of knowledge that many managers have found such processes unhelpful. The statement produced by Peter Honey and myself is both broader and tighter:

'In our view, a manager has learnt something when either or both of the following descriptions apply:

He knows something he did not know earlier and can show it.

He is able to do something he was not able to do before.'[2]

The significance of our definition can be better understood by see-ing it in the context of the other well-known American author on the subject of adult learning, Malcolm Knowles.[3] He articulated what is now recognized to be an important difference between traditional approaches to teaching young people and the ap-proaches necessary to help adults learn. He contrasted the former approach, 'Pedagogy', with 'Andragogy'. While he now regards the two models as parallel rather than antithetical, his valuable insight is about the differences. Essentially he sees the adult learner as a participant instead of simply a recipient. This view is based on the following characteristics of adult learners:

> The learner is self-directed but has a conditioned expectation to be dependent and to be taught.

> The learner comes with experience which means that, for many kinds of learning, adults are themselves the richest resources for one another and that there is a wide range of experience in most groups of learners.

> They are ready to learn when they have a need to perform more effectively in some aspects of their lives.

> For the most part adults do not learn for the sake of learning, they learn in order to be able to perform a task, solve a prob-lem or live in a more satisfying way.

In the United Kingdom, Reg Revans has provided the most impor-tant single statement of learning theory as far as managers are con-cerned.[4] There are substantial similarities with Knowles. To Revans, learning is a specific example of the scientific approach. He describes System Beta involving the assembly of data, the develop-ment of a theory, experimentation, a comparison of results derived from experiments, and the final evaluation of the theory. While this view of the learning process will be particularly attractive to managers with an engineering or scientific base, another aspect of his contribution has all the power of a simple and understand-able model.

This aspect concerns the identification of the difference between what he describes as programmed knowledge and the questioning approach. Programmed knowledge (P) is learning from what someone else has learned, this information being provided in the form of books, papers, studies and lectures. Questioning (Q) is learning from your own processes of action and reflection. This has led to the emphasis on real work rather than simulation, a process called Action Learning. If we look back at previous chapters we can see that Revans's analysis helps to explain some of the responses to the different kinds of learning opportunity offered, particularly the constant refrain of learning from real work.

Knowles and Revans would tend to share the view that too much learning for adults has been directed at knowledge, expressed through the learning processes of memory and understanding, as compared with application of knowledge in either specific or general terms.

Another insight on learning is offered by Chris Argyris.[5] He was concerned to look at both the nature of the learning process and its consequences, being particularly concerned with the problem-solving process – how individuals and organizations recognized and resolved problems. He produced the concept of single loop learning and double loop learning. Single loop learning is the process by which people are enabled to deal with problems as they are currently defined. Double loop learning occurs where individuals or organizations challenge the definition and the circumstances through which the issues requiring learning occur. Single loop learning seems to be appropriate for routine and programmed issues, whereas double loop learning addresses underlying individual and organizational values and assumptions. In his view single loop learning is understandably but unnecessarily limited – necessary but not sufficient.

Not the least valuable contribution made by Argyris is that he identifies the process other people have called 'unlearning'. Managers are sometimes even more reluctant to surrender what they have learned in the past, to recognize that it no longer fits the present, than they are to take aboard new learning. Very often the need for that kind of unlearning arises because someone or something has challenged previous values or processes in the organization. Chapter 7 described in detail how those values and processes normally affect what managers learn and indeed sometimes determine what they learn.

The crucial characteristics of learning for managers as a generalized process are:

The acquisition of knowledge and acting upon it are inextricably intertwined.

It is centred on the wish of the individual to understand, and more particularly to do, something differently or better in managerial terms.

Are learning and development different?

Pedler and Boydell[6] offer a definition of development which resembles the different kinds of learning expressed by Argyris. They feel that development is not just more of something you have already, which might involve increases in your knowledge or a higher degree of an existing skill. 'Development is a different state of being or functioning.'

Their definition also has a great deal in common with that of Revans; there seems a clear correlation between their view of the difference between learning and development and his differentiation between P & Q. Other authors would probably share a similar view that learning is addressed more to issues of definable and immediate concern, whereas development relates more to issues of general competence and future capacity. Indeed some management development schemes and processes use the word 'development' precisely because it is more about general competence and future potential.

A complementary view is offered by a number of writers, particularly from America, who have recognized that managers go through different stages of their lives with different motivation and different consequences. The popular version of the original theory is given in Sheehy.[7] The fact that managers will differ from one another can certainly be analysed, and possible can be better understood by reference to larger scale development processes occurring within the individual. However, while these analyses are interesting and helpful to some individuals, I am not persuaded that there is a significant difference between learning and development in terms of what is actually occurring as distinct from what the objectives and consequences of the processes might be. Both learning and development involve a better understanding of some aspect of your life and then the opportunity to act.

The process of learning

So far we have looked in this chapter at the broad picture of what learning involves for managers. Our next step is to try to understand how and why as far as individuals are concerned there are different versions of this same picture. The main contribution on this was made by David Kolb[1] who produced an illustration (Figure 11.2) describing his total theory of how people learn from experience. Kolb's cycle was:

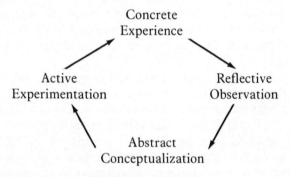

Figure 11.2 Learning from experience

While there are some precursors to this cycle, for example in the work of Kurt Lewin he quotes himself, Kolb's discovery was unique and of fundamental importance. While the cycle represents the ideal and desirable full learning process, Kolb pointed out that not all individuals were equally well equipped to handle each stage of the learning cycle. He then developed a questionnaire through which it was possible to identify which individual had a preference for a particular stage of learning activity (the Learning Styles Inventory). This discovery is of fundamental importance. It will help to explain reactions the learner may have had to certain kinds of learning experience. The learner may then choose either to avoid similar frustrating experiences or to try to develop particular kinds of learning ability in order to take advantage of a wider range of opportunities. For those who are offering learning experiences to managers, particularly management developers, management educators and trainers, this discovery ought to make a big difference in what is offered and how it is offered. Neither the basic facts nor the consequences have yet been accepted. My own development beyond Kolb is shown on page 66 and in the next chapter.

The fact that individuals respond differently to the same kind of learning experience (and indeed to exactly the same learning activity) is evident from our interviews as well as from previous experience. If we take the most structured kind of learning experience, a course, we can test the conclusion about individual differences. Let us presume that two managers are sent on a one-week course 'devising a marketing plan'. They are from the same organization, they are the same age and sex, both have made the personal choice of attending the course (rather than being sent on it) as a result of discussion with their boss about the need to improve one area of management effectiveness. They attend exactly the same course with the same tutors and work in the same group. One manager returns from the course and on the Monday of his return is already starting to put into effect some of the processes described on it. The other manager returns, gives no evidence of taking any action and when questioned about the course utters only those bromide comments expected when an organization has laid out a significant course fee.

Other experiences, less controlled as scientific experiments, support the same conclusion. One manager learns a great deal from attendance at meetings by watching and noting the performance of the most effective participants; another manager with the same kind of opportunity is unable subsequently to quote any of the relevant processes occurring during the meeting. One manager will read an interesting article in the *Harvard Business Review*, mark relevant passages, pass it to his subordinates and discuss with them interesting features of potential application; another manager will carry the same article around in his briefcase for weeks but never actually read it.

It ought not to be a matter of surprise that individuals differ in their reaction to learning processes as they differ in almost every other aspect of thinking about their work. The fact that this common-sense view is ignored in so much of what is offered under the title of management development explains the inefficiency and ineffectiveness of the development offered and achieved. Later in the chapter we shall be looking at ways in which individuals can be helped to understand and perhaps improve their own learning processes.

Learning processes should be designed and offered which cover the full sequence illustrated in the learning cycle. Although individuals may have preferences for particular stages of the cycle (and some are equally at home in all) all can be helped to learn from each stage.

Some management courses try to provide a catholic menu, involving a wide variety of methods, in the hope that parts of it will suit each individual part of the time. Other programmes, for example that of the Harvard Business School, operate differently. There the predominant process is that of the 'case method', whereby managers are presented with detailed case studies, are required to analyse and discuss them and then expose their views to the intellectual analyses of a professor.

Powerful, rigorous and influential though this process can undoubtedly be, when tested against the learning cycle it clearly lacks the stage Kolb called Active Experimentation, and which managers would perhaps describe as implementation. Some courses work even more narrowly, either by providing a great deal of relatively abstract and theoretical information or by providing a lot of action but insufficient time to reflect and generate general conclusions.

The powerful nature of Reg Revans's analysis can be seen particularly clearly by using the Learning Cycle to assess what happens in the Action Learning process. The essence of the latter is that managers work on a real project of concern to themselves and to the organization in which they are working. The project must be real and not invented simply for the purposes of learning.

The first stage of working on the project is that which Kolb calls Concrete Experience. The manager joins other managers involved similarly with their own projects for discussion about his project and the problems and opportunities involved in it. In preparation for the discussion, and as a consequence of it, he is carrying through the Reflective Observation stage. In the third stage managers begin to generate views from these first two stages, generalizing from their experience and identifying guidelines for themselves when engaged in similar activities. This is the Kolb stage of Abstract Conceptualization. Finally, they complete the cycle by applying the results of their learning so far either within the existing project or to future managerial activities.

Examples of the Learning Cycle at work on a particular management task or project were given in Chapters 1 to 4. The cycle itself is illustrated in Figure 2.3. Although the figure shows how learning can be acquired while a task activity occurs, it is possible to think about what might occur and plan to learn in advance, as well as to learn after the event.

Learning - conscious and difficult?

The theories and processes offered so far have the great advantage of being in tune with how managers themselves perceive learning, on the rare occasions when they are asked to think about it. To say however that these processes are within the ability of managers to comprehend is not to say that learning itself is easy. It is natural in the sense that breathing is natural; yet when you learn to swim you have to learn to breathe through a process which is consciously different. Conversion from a learning process which may be natural but is often inefficiently carried out to one which is more aware, more controlled and more effective is not easy.

An illustration is available from a profession, acting, which is much more evidently associated with the need to learn than most managers would probably presume themselves to be. It is from Anthony Sher's description of his approach to the role of Richard III in which he made such a stunning success. 'I think Richard is coming together. A major problem at the moment is a commonplace one - the effort of learning. It is the same when you approach any new skill or technique from a dance to driving a car. The effort of learning stops you, at first, from doing well'.[8]

How conscious the learning process is, expecially while a manager is engaged in a particular activity, is debatable. There can even be debate about how consciously the manager must undertake a review of what has happened in order to learn from it. Some managers are less likely than others to be able to undertake this reflective process from a predisposition to learn that way. While however there can be arguments about the proportion or extent of consciousness required, the thrust of this book is to show how much more can be achieved by consciously planning learning beforehand, understanding learning experience while it is happening and reviewing it subsequently. For many managers normal managerial life does not accommodate itself to this kind of process. Managers understand that their managerial life is lived forwards; perhaps they understand less well that their learning life is experienced backwards.

Influences on learning

In earlier chapters we looked at opportunities for learning particularly on the job but also those which can be designed or created outside it. We reviewed also what directors do and how it influences both learning opportunities and learning practices. Similarly we looked at factors outside the job such as the nature of the organization itself, its culture and purposes as a further explanation of the context in which learning occurs. Figure 11.3 shows the large number of factors influencing learning.

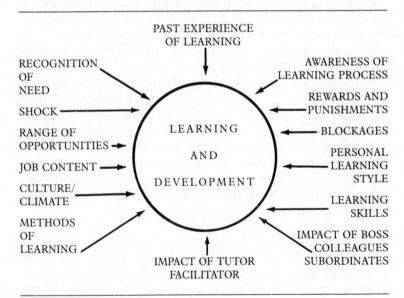

Figure 11.3 Influences on learning

The figure immediately illustrates an obvious characteristic about individual learners; they differ from each other in their capacity to recognize and take advantage of learning opportunities. One aspect of this follows from the Learning Cycle theory identified earlier. Individuals are not all equipped with the capacity to learn effectively at each stage of the cycle. Some individuals are happy when engaged in direct activity, but much less happy when asked to think about what they have learned from the activity. Some individuals accept new information or new experience only when it is accompanied by some model, structure or theory; others have little concern for underlying theory but a great deal for whether a management practice can be applied in their particular circumstance. In the next chapter processes for helping managers to identify whether they have a strong preference for learning a particular way are discussed.

Some writers would include 'motivation' in an analysis of influences. In Figure 11.3 the identifiable aspects of motivation are shown separately, particularly:

> Rewards and Punishments
> Recognition of Need
> Shock

The idea of rewards and punishments is easily understood, not least because it applies to all kinds of management activities and not just to learning. Managers may expect to be rewarded if they learn or punished if they do not. This would apply if for example an individual was seen as being insufficiently effective in handling management accounts. The positive reward might be that the manager would be better equipped to do the job required, while the negative punishment would occur if he was shown up in front of colleagues or boss as failing to understand the accounts. One problem however is that such relatively clear relationships between something a manager wants to do well and a desire to learn may not be present. The perceived reward from learning may actually be low from the manager's point of view, either because the need to learn has not been clearly established or because the actual issue involved seems remote from current reality. Some managers, for example, perceive little benefit and therefore little reward from sessions about the British Economy.

Another important aspect of reward is the element of risk

involved in learning; trying to learn something new implies the possibility of failing to learn. Unless the perceived reward of attempting to learn is relatively high, managers may choose to avoid the risk. On the other hand for some individuals or in some circumstances the expectation of reward may be lower than a fear of punishment as a result of taking the risk of learning. The attempt to learn something new, to change a previous style of behaviour, may be experienced as uncomfortable and lowering of the individual's self-perception of competence.

Finally there is the issue of short-term versus long-term reward. Managers who accept a difficult job posting, or who take an MBA, may in different ways be expecting reward in the long term for engaging in that particular kind of learning activity.

Recognition of needs

The concept of rewards is tied up with whether a manager recognizes a need to learn something. In our survey, the two were sometimes combined in the manager's mind by an initial recognition that he had a weakness and then a belief that he would gain some reward for overcoming it. The need to learn may be either highly specific or more general in the sense that a manager sets a career goal and believes that a particular learning process might help towards it. The processes by which managers sort out needs for themselves are set out later.

Shock

We found a number of directors for whom the learning and development process had been relatively sequential, with blocks of learning built on one another with at least a resemblance to a Cotswold stone wall if not to a highly uniform brick wall. We also found cases where directors had learned through some great leap. Sometimes this was being thrown into a totally new job in a quite different environment, sometimes a dramatic change within a relatively familiar job and environment. This kind of quantum leap could be seen as the occasion for learning (when it happened) or the cause of learning (in retrospect). In all probability it is the combination of the two which provides a dramatic impetus to the learning process. The kind of upset or disequilibrium which arises from time to time in organizations, in turn leading to an awareness on the part of an individual that some new approach or activity is required, can often stimulate such a change. The phenomenon of shock is to be seen in the progression of directors through a number of jobs. Gabarro[9] shows that there are five stages in a manager taking over a new job:

Taking Hold
Immersion
Reshaping
Consolidation
Refinement

Each of these lasts for different periods depending on the person and the situation. The learning process also varies according to the stage involved. In the first stage, taking hold, you may have to learn about the product, the people, the problem and perhaps even about the organization if you have joined from outside. As one of our interviewees said, 'The problem is you have to keep the business running while you are learning about it'. While at this early stage you learn to deal with the most obvious factors, you begin later on to learn in order to deal with the less obvious issues, patterns and conflicts. Only at the final stage, refinement, does learning become relatively incremental and routine rather than novel.

There is one theory of motivation which draws together a number of the influences which I have separated for clarity in Figure 11.3. Handy[10] uses the concept of 'motivation calculus':

1   The strength or salience of the need.
2   The expectancy that energy or effort will lead to a particular result.
3   The instrumentality of that result in producing the need shown at (1).

The significance of this is that while a manager may believe he has a need, and expect to be rewarded for trying to learn, he may still not believe in a particular process if he does not see the likelihood of a connection between the learning process offered and the desired earned result. An example of this would be:

A manager might see the need to improve his organization's approach to competition.

He might believe that collecting experience from other people would be a good way of adding to his knowledge.

He might believe that reading the book *Competitive Strategy* by Porter would help satisfy the need.

If the manager's need is not very strong, he is unlikely to undertake any work to satisfy it. On the other hand, he may have a strong need but feel that the nature of his particular organization is unique and that therefore it is unlikely he will learn anything from looking at the approach of other people. Finally he may have a strong need in the sense of a general belief that help from outside might be useful, but actually not believe that a textbook even by the famous Professor Porter would help him because, he believes, it is largely based on American experience.

Blockages to learning and development

Some of the influences mentioned may of course be experienced as either positive or negative. It is especially important to look at the things which block learning, because so much learning is inefficient. Figure 11.4 draws on the work of Temporal and Boydell.[11]

The item 'Expressive' is worth elaboration because it brings out a fundamental point about learning not so far discussed. A manager may be unable to describe what he or she is doing or feeling, lacking the ability to set out clearly the nature of a problem. The probability is that the manager will then not be able to get help on the problem from other people, and will lose the opportunity to learn from them. The problem of such people was illustrated for me many years ago in a film I saw in which the managerial character, after many attempts to communicate his point, shouted 'Don't listen to what I say, listen to what I mean'.

It may seem odd to those brought up to envisage the learning process as essentially about teaching that we should identify communication skills in the learner, rather than in the teacher, as significant. However, our emphasis throughout this book has been on learning from the reality of what managers do, and it is precisely

Perceptual	– Not seeing there is a problem
Cultural	– The way things are here . . .
Emotional	– Fear or insecurity
Motivational	– Unwillingness to take risk
Cognitive	– Poor previous learning experience
Intellectual	– Limited learning styles
	– Poor learning skills
Expressive	– Poor communication skills
Situational	– Lack of opportunities
Physical	– Wrong place, time
Specific environment	– Boss/colleagues unsupportive

Figure 11.4 Blocks to learning

in that situation that the issue of expressive skill emerges. The manager who could not interpret management accounts would certainly enhance his ability to get help if he could explain clearly the particular areas of difficulty.

Expressive skills, or the lack of them, can be seen particularly clearly where the learning interaction is essentially large scale in a group rather than one to one. In real managerial life managers work a great deal of the time in groups, in which their ability to explain what they mean is important both managerially, in the sense of task performance, and in terms of learning, for the reasons mentioned above. Similarly, on training courses the capacity to exchange and develop ideas with colleagues is a very significant contributor to effective learning. Course attenders constantly say that they learn more from interaction with others on the course than they do from formal sessions. Although this may sometimes be a comment on the quality of formal sessions, a great deal of learning undoubtedly occurs within the group. However, if individuals cannot explain themselves, their problems and what they have to offer the group, the chances of getting effective response are reduced, and therefore learning is reduced (although not of course eliminated since they can learn from others if they can at least listen effectively).

Learning as a social process

The power of groups to influence each other's performance can be seen in such groups as Weight Watchers, Alcoholics Anonymous and Gamblers Anonymous. Here we see the provision of support to participants in the group, providing encouragement to achieve a defined objective. We also see the powerful fear of embarrassment in that so long as someone is prepared to continue attending he or she is motivated not to eat, drink or gamble by the fact of having to stand up and tell the truth. In the same way learning groups can be powerful motivators of continued learning amongst participants. For example the use of learning logs mentioned on page 205 can be both enhanced by exchanges about the content of logs between members of the group, and also sustained by group pressure because members of a learning group will be reluctant to confess that they have failed to complete their log.

This reinforces a general proposition about the individual learner, which is that for many activities the learner will need support from some source, which may be the boss, colleagues, spouse, tutor or adviser. This is the public face of learning. However for some activities, and particularly for some learners, some aspects of learning will be private, not shared with others. These will be governed by introspection, a process we call Reflection in learning.

Summary

A manager's willingness to learn is most often specific rather than general, related to a performance requirement rather than to a detached interest in a piece of knowledge. That willingness is increased or diminished by various influences, the most identifiable being those centred on the job itself and on people important to the manager.

An interest in learning does not mean that an individual manager will respond to a particular opportunity or process. Individuals have differing levels of willingness to learn through particular processes and different styles of learning. The next chapter pursues these themes.

References

1   Kolb, D., *Experiential Learning*, Prentice-Hall, Englewood Cliffs, New Jersey, 1984

2   Honey, P. and Mumford, A., *Manual of Learning Styles* and *Using Your Learning Styles*, Honey, 2nd ed., London 1986

3   Knowles, M., *Androgyny in Action*, Jossey Bass, San Francisco, 1985

4   Revans, R., *Action Learning*, Blond, London, 1980

5   Argyris, C., *Reasoning, Learning and Action*, Jossey Bass, San Francisco, 1982

6   Pedler, M. and Boydell, T., *Managing Yourself*, Fontana, London, 1986

7   Sheehy, G., *Passages*, Bantam, New York, 1977

8   Sher, A., *Year of the King*, Methuen, London, 1986

9   Gabarro, J., 'When a new manager takes charge', *Harvard Business Review*, May/June 1985, pp. 110–23

10   Handy, C., *Understanding Organisations*, Penguin Books, London, 1985

11   Temporal, P. and Boydell, T., *Helping Managers to Learn*, Sheffield City Polytechnic, Sheffield, 1981

12 Learning and development: methods

Earlier chapters described the experiences of managers on the way to becoming directors. Figure 12.1 shows the main processes available (although there are scores of variants). The vast majority of people we saw had experienced some of these processes. The reason they had not encountered others was partly lack of opportunity. Not all had been exposed for example to courses employing a range of teaching procedures; although all had experienced some form of accidental learning not all had been involved in many of the controlled development processes on the job.

Some learning methods are not appropriate to particular kinds of learning need. The idea of a process being good in itself with no reference to what the learning process is intended to achieve is nonsensical, even without the recognition of different individual approaches to learning. It is now much less likely than it once was that managers will be sent on programmes about interviewing skills in which they are exposed to lectures, books and perhaps film without ever themselves undertaking interviewing role play. The view that if the intention is to help somebody improve a skill you need to provide an opportunity for the skill to be first shown and then developed on a course is scarcely new. Certainly for off-the-job processes, it is now quite possible to assess the need (for a skill knowledge), to review the list of available methods and try to provide the process best suited.

This judgement becomes slightly more complex when a particular situation is considered. Whereas in a course, for example,

Off the job	*On the job*
Books	Modelling
Lectures	Coaching
Programmed learning	Counselling
Interactive video	Demonstration
Films	Experiment
Group discussion	Accident
Case study	Process consultation
In-tray	Self-diagnostic instruments
Business games	Algorithms
Sumulations	Assignments
T groups	Secondments
Demonstration and practice	Projects
Role plays	
Outdoor	
Discovery	
Diagnostic instruments	

Figure 12.1 Methods of learning

role plays will normally be designed and operated with some care, they are sometimes used in real management situations quite effectively but in a wholly off-the-cuff form. The manager will simply say to his subordinate: 'You present the managerial case, and I will be the Trade Union representative.' On a course, feedback about the role play will often be conducted either by a professional trainer supposedly equipped to give feedback in an acceptable form, or by colleagues on the course who have been shown what is involved in effective feedback. In contrast feedback about role plays in the real managerial situation is not normally centred on the learning process but on the task involved – with reduced learning benefits in many cases.

Another way of making an appropriate choice of methods in relation to the skill or competency required is to group the skills. I have carried out two diagnostic studies of organizations moving into a matrix or programme management organizational system. In some respects the changes required for effective performance by managers are well represented by the concept of shock mentioned in the previous chapter. The more specific changes involved included:

>to understand better the purposes and methods of working of other parts of the business

>to change concepts of how the organization system should be defined in order to be effective

>to develop skills in confronting issues and resolving conflict rather than sustaining old conflicts, for example between design and manufacturing

>to be willing to take initiatives and sustain risks and potential damage at an individual level by changing behaviour

Within this change to matrix management managers were required both to understand and to carry out certain managerial processes. They needed not only to understand 'What are the main features of matrix management?' but also the specific behaviour necessary to carry through the reorganization. A process which emphasized the former had been found to be largely ineffective; a subsequent design which combined the conceptual issues with the opportunity to work on particular behaviour such as listening effectively to people to whom you are not used to listening was much more effective.

Even if we were to concentrate simply on appropriateness and methods, therefore, we can see that appropriateness has no general validity. It is a judgement which can be made only after reviewing:

>the range of possible methods

>the content of the issue on which learning is desired

>the particular situation or opportunity in which learning may occur

However, as has already been suggested, this three-stage approach is complicated by the impertinence of individuals who operate their own choices about the processes from which they will learn most effectively, which may mean that they refuse to accept the process theoretically best suited to the need because they happen not to learn best that way.

Knowing your needs

It was clear from descriptions offered to us in our survey that most of the directors had not learned through a carefully analysed controlled and directed learning process. Most of them had learned through a combination of accidental, opportunistic and occasionally well-structured learning experiences. The thesis we developed was that accidental processes would probably continue to predominate, and that more use could be made of accidents in a slightly more planned opportunistic way, integrating them into real management processes. Such an approach however is a supplement to, not a replacement for, more carefully planned approaches to learning.

The planning should start with an individual job review. The individual looks at the demands of his or her job, reviewing the situation in which the job has been performed. The manager carries out an inventory of areas of effectiveness in the job, and conducts a self-appriasal of performance against them. Deliberately this process has been described as starting with the person occupying the job; in many organizations that self-review would be followed or perhaps preceded by a review by the manager's boss.

The process of appraising managerial performance, usually accompanied by a section on the appraisal form which asks those involved to identify training needs and often to identify answers as well, is familiar by now in most organizations in the UK, at least in manufacturing and commerce.

As already suggested, however, even a careful identification of needs, and the kind of solution to those needs which will probably result from a discussion between a line manager and a management development adviser, may still not produce the most effective answer. Given the range of possible influences on a manager's learning, the bland assumption inherent in most of these appraisal processes that needs will be properly identified and appropriate solutions defined can only be put down to an unfortunate combination of naïvety and ignorance.

Establishing learning preferences

It is a crazily inefficient process to throw managers into learning opportunities without serious consideration of whether they are likely to learn from them. What kind of manager is likely to benefit most from being selected to participate in a task group on some current organizational concern? Who is most likely to benefit from attending a high-level post-education management programme? Who will respond to a computerized business exercise as a brilliant simulation of reality, and who will dismiss it as a 'game'?

It is a substantial criticism of the centres of excellence for management learning that they seem to have taken a typically production-oriented view of the processes they offer; essentially they sell a product with little concern for the processes through which the customer responds to the product. They fail even to discuss the very process, learning, in which their student customers are involved. Only in recent years have the efforts of a few academics and practitioners caught up with the reality recognized long ago by managers, that one manager learns well from a process from which another will not learn. Moreover managers have operated on this understanding, for example by saying that Peter Brown should not go on a particular course because he would not learn from it, or by finding ways themselves of avoiding inappropriate learning oportunitites. It is now possible, however, to help managers to assess the likelihood of them learning from a particular process.

The most open-ended approach is that of 'learning biography', which involves asking managers to describe, for example, the two most significant and the two least influential learning experiences in their lives. As well as being productive of group discussion, such a process can help individuals to determine which learning processes are most helpful to them, and why.

In our work in the International Management Centre from Buckingham we combine this learning biography with a much more detailed analysis of the individual's learning preferences, using a Learning Styles Questionnaire. There is no doubt that provided the process is attached to an end valued by the manager, and is not simply deployed as an interesting exercise with no apparent purpose, discussion of learning history and Learning Styles is a powerful and helpful process.

The Learning Styles approach we use is that designed by Honey and Mumford[1] following the original ground-breaking discoveries of David Kolb mentioned earlier. Our Learning Styles Questionnaire is designed to assess four Learning Styles which can be sharply differentiated both in principle and in practice. The questionnaire is based primarily on managerial behaviour and not on learning behaviour, but leads to conclusions about predicted responses to particular kinds of learning activity. The four styles, with some illustrations of learning processes are:

Activists will learn best from activities where:
> They can engross themselves in the short here-and-now activities such as business games and competitive teamwork tasks.
> They are thrown in at the deep end with a task they think is difficult.

They learn less from and may react against activities where:
> Learning involves a passive role, eg listening to lectures, reading.
> They are offered statements they see as theoretical, ie explanation of cause or background.

Reflectors learn best from activities where:
> They are able to stand back from events and listen and observe.
> They are asked to produce carefully considered analyses and reports.

They learn less well from activities where:
> They are involved in situations which require action without planning.
> They are worried by time pressures or rushed from one activity to another.

Theorists learn best from activities where:
> What is being offered is part of a system, model, concept or theory.

They are offered interesting ideas and concepts even though they are not immediately relevant.

They learn less well from activities where:
They are involved in unstructured activities where ambiguity and uncertainty are great.
They feel themselves out of tune with other participants especially when of a lower intellectual calibre.

Pragmatists learn best from activities where:
There is an obvious link between the subject matter and the problem or opportunity on the job.
They are exposed to a model they can emulate, eg respected boss, a film showing how it is done.

They learn less well from activities where:
The learning event seems distant from reality
There is no practice or clear guidelines on how to do it.

Note: These are illustrations only of a much wider list of preferred learning activities.

The Learning Styles Questionnaire has now been used and validated in practice not only by the authors but by many subsequent users with thousands of managers. In our survey of directors the answers showed not only the familiar spread of preferences but also some strong associations between the comments made by directors in the discussions about their learning experiences and the scores achieved in the Learning Styles Questionnaire. In our research with the general managerial population who had completed the LSQ produced similar findings. Some directors had a strong attachment to one style, as had about 35 per cent of managers. They would be predicted to learn well from only a restricted range of learning activities related to their basic learning style preference, as compared with the 20 per cent of managers who had high scores on three of the learning style preferences and therefore would be predicted to learn well from a wide variety of activities. These predictions were borne out when we analysed what the directors themselves said about satisfying and unsatisfying learning experiences.

The point of establishing learning style preferences however is not to establish that individuals differ from one another but to do something about that fact. There are two different lines to follow. The first is to say that knowledge of your own preferred learning style enables you to make a better choice, if one is available, between different kinds of learning opportunities. Thus while an Activist might enjoy, participate full in and even learn something from an outdoor management training course, a person with particularly strong Theorist or Reflector scores ought to think twice about it. Similarly, the manager quoted earlier who wanted to know more about competitive strategy might, if an Activist, decide that learning from a book was an unfruitful venture.

The logic of this line of thought is that if a manager decided from a review of job-centred needs that he had a particular learning requirement, he could then review those needs in the context of the wide range of opportunities mentioned in the first four chapters. However, this choice might sensibly be influenced by the additional knowledge gained from the Learning Styles Questionnaire on which kind of opportunity might be most likely to be effective.

There is a further thread to be drawn from the knowledge of learning preferences. These are not immutable, unchanged by particular situations or time. It is quite possible for a manager to make deliberate attempts to increase versatility as a learner, as Honey and Mumford have shown.[1] This will certainly not happen merely by being exposed to a questionnaire, scores and comparison with norms. It can happen if a manager is helped either directly by a counsellor or by a work book. This discussion of preferred approaches to learning has deliberately been interpolated into the analysis of needs, because needs do not exist solely as needs *for* learning but as needs *about* learning.

Analysing needs

Let us not return to the original theme – analysing needs for learning. Many directors in our survey lacked any help in establishing neither their actual levels of performance in required areas of competence, or how their often somewhat vague view that they ought not to stop learning could be converted into something more specific. Whereas at lower and middle levels of management the deficiencies of appraisal systems are in some cases being remedied by the introduction of assessment centres, with carefully established criteria for performance, such intimate processes are not available to people at the top. Indeed at the lower levels, in some of the more progressive organizations, assessment centres are used not merely to assess selection but also to assess people in development terms, ie to establish what skill they need to improve and how to improve it.

At the top level there is a need for a more individualized approach. One way would be to use Henry Mintzberg's analysis of the managerial role as the basis for self-assessment.[2] On which do you think yourself a strong performer, on which do you think yourself less effective?

An alternative approach is one which I used as an internal consultant some years ago[3] and which we found in our survey was used by another organization through an external consultant. The process deploys an experienced and credible counsellor to discuss performance and development needs with senior managers with a view to producing a development plan.

The kind of analysis I used was: (a) personal background, (b) experience and skill (involving a review of managerial experience perhaps in different functions), (c) own perception of strength, (d) own perception of areas for improvement, (e) current personal development needs, (f) needs for future identified role, (g) career ambition. The purpose of these analytical activities, singly or in combination, is to produce an awareness of development needs and a willingness to seek development opportunities.

A subsequent willingness to take direct responsibility for your own development has been given the title 'self-development'. The acceptance of responsibility by the individual as the prime participant in a process of development, rather than the recipient of someone else's planned teaching, is one of the three main phenomena of management development over the last 15 years. (The others are Action Learning and Learning Styles.) This concept and many practical exercises presenting alternatives to those described here are provided in Pedler and Burgoyne.[4] It is a fundamental and difficult shift from a process 'done to' managers to a process in which management development is 'done with' managers. I describe it as follows:

Responsibility for learning is taken on by the learner and not seen as the responsibility of the provider of the learning opportunities.

The emphasis is on the individual and his or her particular needs rather than on large groups of managers with general needs.

The manager is not simply judged by other people on his or her learning needs and solutions to them but rather is involved in the analysis of needs and the discussion of solutions.

Because of the process of involvement, responsibility rests with the learner, leaving him or her with fewer excuses about the relevance of applicability of solutions to supposed needs.

The combination of involvement and responsibility generates commitment to personal action, instead of acceptance of the need to follow someone else's prescription.

Because the individual works on designing needs for himself as a person, he has already begun to engage not only in the generation of solutions but in work on the solutions. The sometimes unhelpful distinction between analysis and action is reduced.

This section has been about acquiring more knowledge about yourself, taking more responsibility for that self and for the processes of development to be chosen. This however does not imply that the analysis of needs, and even less working on solutions, should be a solitary process. We know that others contribute greatly to our self-knowledge and to our ability to improve ourselves. Sadly we know too little about how this is actually achieved except that it involves experiences of exchange and feedback. The precise nature of those exchanges is too little understood, but some fascinating insights are given in Stuart.[5]

The skills of learning

The study of Learning Styles reveals that individuals may be strong or weak in particular kinds of learning skills. If I were not already aware of the extraordinary lack of interest in learning processes I would be surprised that I had encountered no alternative view about skills to the one I offered in 1980.[6] I now take the view that the list represents a total ideal and is perhaps rather too formidable for most practising managers. The list should therefore be seen as something to be borne in mind rather than as a complete objective.

Skills involved in effective learning behaviour

The ability to establish effective criteria for yourself
The ability to measure your effectiveness
The ability to identify your own learning needs
The ability to plan personal learning
The ability to take advantage of learning opportunities
The ability to review your own learning processes
The ability to listen to others
The capacity to accept help
The ability to face unwelcome information
The ability to take risks and tolerate anxieties
The ability to analyse what other successful performers do
The ability to know yourself
The ability to share information with others
The ability to review what has been learned

I would now for example take the view that the ability to analyse what other successful performers do is desirable but not totally necessary. On the other hand the ability to know yourself, by which I meant the ability to see a gap between yourself as you are and yourself as you need to be, is wholly necessary at least in the conscious learning mode.

Planning the future

It is much easier to utter a cliché about learning being a lifelong process than to understand what this means, and it is even less easy to put the concept into operation. If it is to be more than an accidental process, it surely involves the kind of understanding about the self as learner which has been described. Learning to learn must itself be part of any organized development process. As I have commented earlier, this may be a shattering conclusion for the providers of many management training and education courses who at the moment do not accept this proposition. My own institution puts its syllabus where my mouth is, firstly by requiring specific attention to learning on our major programmes; secondly by building in 'learning to learn' processes as a continuing part of our training; and thirdly on our MBA programme by requiring that continued membership of IMCB is subject to confirmation five years later only if the manager can show that learning has continued.

The process which we encourage is the use of a learning log or diary. The note of guidance we give to our participants includes the following suggestions:

Make notes of what happened, 'I tried to do Y', 'X in making his point seemed to'. These notes should record rather than comment. Record next your comments and conclusions; these should concentrate on what *you* have learned. List direction points saying what you are going to do and when. Your action points will be most effective if they are:

> clear
> specific
> setting out behaviour rather that attitudes
> realistic, ie going for small manageable actions rather than
>   large-scale grand designs.

This kind of process is one which Reflectors will more naturally follow. It may however be more interesting to quote from someone whose style was predominantly Activist. The discipline of keeping a log-book was, he found, useful precisely because it caused him to think about some of the uncomfortable issues and unresolved problems he was exposed to both on his MBA programme and in his work life.

It is of course easier to include this kind of process within a formal learning programme, to set aside time for it and to monitor achievement on it. While there are some people who will enjoy the process afterwards on the same basis that some people like writing a personal diary, the majority of managers probably need some additional reward beyond the pleasure of talking to themselves. The answer is to share some of the thoughts and consequences of your learning log with one or more colleagues, in precisely the same was as we have suggested earlier for other kinds of learning process. The reward of sharing with other people, getting comments on your problems, perhaps helping them with theirs, is part of the process of group encouragement and support which is generally desirable in learning.

One way to continue interest and development is to find different approaches to analysing your own performance and development processes. A manager might want, for example, to turn to the left/right brain analysis, or the Myers Briggs inventory of personality types. These are not recommended here as a first course of action because they are one step removed from the explicit behaviour which I believe to be the most useful thing to work on. They are however interesting and thoughtful approaches which might usefully stimulate action at a subsequent stage.

Organizational learning

The work of Chris Argyris was quoted on page 180. Although I find his concepts of single and double loop learning meaningful, I believe Argyris is actually writing about organizational impacts on individual learning rather than about organizational learning. It is in any event difficult to separate the mass of individuals and their learning from the organization as a mass and its learning. We have seen in Chapter 9 how culture, strategy, structure and environment influence the learning of individuals. They also influence the larger entity and indeed comprise the organization itself. The organization has a culture, myth, a way of doing things which has been created by the interaction of the organization with all the things which influence the way it behaves. The organization or elements within it act and learn from their actions; just like individuals they observe the actions of other organizations, learn from them and sometimes act on that learning. They sometimes attempt to model themselves on other organizations, for example through management books like *In Search of Excellence*. Or they acquire second-hand learning through exchanges between directors on courses or on committees.

As with individuals one of the main problems can be that of unlearning, putting aside often hard-earned experience and wisdom which no longer matches current circumstances. Organizations are set up to learn effectively even more rarely than individuals. They may monitor the outside environment, but they rarely set up processes for monitoring the learning from their own internal activities; the monitoring activity is task focused and not applied to the meaning of success or failure in learning terms.

If we return to Argyris however we can usefully remember the distinction between single and double loop learning. Like individuals most organizations are better (though still badly) equipped for single loop learning, doing better that which they do within the context and values already accepted by the organization. Double loop learning within an organization, challenging and changing its norms and values, learning how this is to be achieved and learning from the no doubt flawed achievement of it, has been identified by some theorists as a useful process but not yet widely implemented.

The vital point about organizational learning is that learning for managers is a social process, and is therefore responsive to group processes and to an overall organizational climate. My colleague Peter Honey uses an organizational climate approach in which he says that an organization encourages learning if:

> it encourages managers to identify their own learning needs and sets challenging learning goals;
> it encourages managers to experiment;
> it provides opportunities for learning both on and off the job;
> it gives on-the-spot feedback;
> it allows time for managers to plan, review and conclude learning activities;
> it tolerates some mistakes, provided managers try to learn from them.

The significance of Peter Honey's list seems to be that it is the expression of the individual behaviour of managers towards colleagues and subordinates. It embodies an approach by which for example rewards of recognition of need, and the provision of a range of opportunities, impact on the individual manager.

The challenge of change

The processes given most emphasis have been those that involve a more effective use of existing experience. There is so much productivity to be gained in this area; there are so many ignored opportunities, so many failures to make effective use of real managerial experience. This is the most immediate and most practical priority. For people on their way to the top, however, and those already there, the challenge of learning will often also be to move outside existing experience, which must in many ways be limited. Learning how to change an organization's culture and objectives, for example, and to change the way in which managers behave within it, may not be easy within the existing processes and values of an organization.

It is for this reason that stretching experiences outside, particularly through well-structured and relevant management training and education programmes, are not only desirable but essential. Managers should make more effective use of the learning experiences available in the current context, and for many this is the first priority. This is not to imply that the challenge of stretching experiences outside that context is not also a very desirable priority for many managers.

References

1   Honey, P. and Mumford, A., *Manual of Learning Styles*, Honey, London, 1986
2   Mintzberg, H., *The Nature of Managerial Work*, Prentice-Hall, Englewood Cliffs, New Jersey, 1980
3   Mumford, A., 'Counselling senior managers' development' in T. Boydell (ed.) and M. Pedler *Management Self Development*, Gower, 1981
4   Pedler, M. and Burgoyne, J., *A Manager's Guide to Self Development*, 2nd ed., McGraw-Hill, Maidenhead, 1986
5   Stuart, R., 'Using others to learn' in A. Mumford (ed.) *Handbook of Management Development*. 2nd edn., Gower, 1986
6   Mumford, A., *Making Experience Pay*, McGraw-Hill, Maidenhead, 1980

Part III

The Way Forward

The two final chapters provide a convenient summary of the actions to be taken by directors, managers and advisers to improve their personal contribution to the development of themselves and others. These chapters are directly descriptive and are challenging and innovatory while still resting on the bedrock of reality.

These chapters may be all that a busy director or manager can read – or they may whet the appetite to read the earlier chapters.

13 Action for executives

This book has discussed a variety of different processes by which managers and directors can learn more effectively. The three basic themes have been:

Look at the job, and the requirements for effective performance in it.

Look at actual performance in the job, and decide whether some parts of that performance might be improved through learning.

Look at the variety of opportunities for learning within and outside the job.

If this sequence were followed the manager or director would be going down a neatly organized and rationally purposive path. They would in fact be following a Type 3 approach to Management Development. However, the argument has been that very often development will not follow this ordered sequence, but will occur as the result of someone spotting a learning opportunity within a task without having previously thought analytically in terms of required job performance and development needs. That is part of the reason why the term 'opportunistic' has been applied to the Type 2 Management development process. The idea here is to take advantage by some planning, thought and reflection of managerial activities perhaps before they happen, but more likely during and after.

Type 3 and Type 2 development are not antagonistic or mutually exclusive. Both are necessary in any organization, and for any individual, where there is a desire to get better organizational and personal results. In this chapter, however, for reasons of relevance and prevalence, more illustrations are given of Type 2 Management Development than Type 3.

The suggestions in this chapter are illustrative; the intention is to highlight the most important or potentially stimulating activities mentioned earlier. If successful with these, an individual might want to return to the earlier chapters to find further nuggets of gold.

While some might be persuaded to consider an activity purely for reasons of self-satisfaction and personal development, most will be motivated by the wish to improve individual and organizational performance. That emphasis on performance both justifies and provides the focus for the kind of activities described here. The wish to manage things well is the father of a learning process which works through managing.

That process provides a double value operation, as compared with the single value achieved through managing a separate learning process.

The story so far ...

The directors we interviewed generally felt that the learning experiences which had significantly contributed to their skills as directors had:

> been closely integrated with current job performance and the needs of the business;
> emerged from accountability in a real job;
> resulted from their being stretched, confidence and competence having been enhanced.

The experiences which were less effective as learning occurred when:

> learning was seen as an end in itself, separate from the reality of management;
> emphasis was on increased knowledge rather than improved ability to 'get things done';
> there had been insufficient recognition at the time of the opportunities to learn from a particular job experience.

Actions for chief executives

We deliberately saw only executive directors in our survey. Fifty-five carried the title chairman, chief executive or managing director, but in some cases the title referred to their role in running an activity as part of their main board responsibility. We saw in fact 21 individuals who were unquestionably at the topmost position in their organization, which we defined as reporting to no other executive director. In terms of their own develpoment on the way to the top there was no measurable difference between this group and the other 123 as a group.

Are chief executives learners?

In Chapter 3 I commented that the findings of Bennis[1] if taken at face value suggest a different view. He says of the leaders he talked to that 'nearly all are highly proficient at learning from experience'. They are said to be perpetual learners, some of them voracious readers and many of them learning from other people such as politicians, academics and customers. According to him they see learning as the essential fuel for their activities in stretching, growing and breaking new ground. They are also said to be very good at using mistakes as learning experiences. It is not clear from the book how far Bennis's 90 leaders matched our 21 chief executives in the sense of sole responsibility at the top; they included orchestral conductors and sports coaches. However, compared with our directors the people he talked to would be exceptionally good learners. It would not be true that our group of chief executives were highly proficient at 'learning from experience' even in terms of their own understanding of what that process involved. I do not know what process Bennis used to establish the comments he made. While it would be comforting to accept what he says, or perhaps what his participants said about themselves, I prefer to rely on our evidence in this area.

While not claiming for themselves any special proficiency in learning, a number of the chief executives we saw indicated interesting processes through which it was still taking place. (They differed in this respect from Lee Iacocca, whose quoted learning experiences all occurred before he became Chief Executive of Chrysler, or so his autobiography suggests since he mentions nothing after reaching that eminence.)

One characteristic of the management hierarchy is that when you reach the top there are very few people in whom you feel it possible to confide. The problem of loneliness affects a number of aspects of the chief executive's job, and influences opportunities to learn. The potential for sharing and learning with others, available even to other main board directors, is reduced for the chief executive.

Learning outside

The way in which chief executives acquire both awareness and ability is a learning process, though they may not be wholly conscious of this. However, several of the chief executives we saw were aware of the need to collect new ideas, to compare processes, to test their problems and solutions against other organizations and other executives at the same level. Chief executives were no more likely than other directors to be voracious readers. The ways in which they met these needs were:

meeting other chief executives on industrial or governmental committees

participation on boards of other companies

One chief executive described how interesting he had found the experience of being a director of another organization, actually working on a quite different part of commercial life. He had observed and reflected on the way in which the board was managed, and as a result of this had noticed things about the processes on his own board of which he had previously been unaware.

What may be thought an extreme case illustrating how a chief executive may 'recharge' is given by Stieglitz.[2] He quotes M. Lecerf, chief executive of a French company, who after nine years as chairman and chief executive took a one-year leave of absence before returning to run the company. He set himself four goals for this year which involved a great deal of travel around the world. Two of the goals were explicitly learning goals:

better knowledge of the international environment

developing ideas on company strategy and guidelines for the future

M. Lecerf comments that he believes he may have indeed generated new ideas not only about direction but about the processes to be used in management.

While the reaction of most chief executives would predictably be astonishment that a chief executive could take a whole year off, the principle is one which might well be attractive to some. Several chief executives commented that there was a significant difficulty in getting the space to think about important business problems. Indeed one said that the issue really was having enough time to decide whether there *were* such problems; while a good chief executive certainly did not spend all his time fire-fighting, it was almost inevitable that he dealt with the obvious agenda. He compared his own experience with that of some managers under him, who had returned from a course with challenging ideas about the organization, its direction and processes. He was doubtful about attending a course himself, but did feel the need to generate some space in which to think, and the need to get some people to help him fill the space with good and useful thinking.

It was surprising how little use directors as a whole seemed to make of the alternative experiences and wisdom presumably available from their non-executive-director colleagues. Perhaps they were reluctant to acknowledge their help for some reason of status or self-consciousness. Yet some of them would refer to learning from executive colleagues on the board. Perhaps it was more to do with the infrequency and relative formality of the meetings with non-executive directors. Perhaps status and infrequency combined to make it less likely that a chief executive would use non-executive colleagues in this way.

Chapter 5 referred to one chief executive who learned quite a lot from actually sharing a session on one of his company's internal management training courses with a high quality academic. Several other chief executives referred to the informal learning they derived from delivering lectures and responding to questions on such programmes. This learning is much more likely to be about the attitudes of others than things the chief executive could improve in his own personal performance.

We encountered one chief executive who had shared with all his colleagues on the board the experience of attending two shortened versions of courses which were to be presented to managers below them. He and they seemed to have benefited significantly, but it may be an experience more likely in a relatively new organization moving into management training for the first time than one with existing training programmes. The actions a chief executive might take to ensure his own continued development are not otherwise significantly different from those suggested later for subordinate colleagues on the main board.

The chief executive and directors

The influence of the chief executive on the development of main board colleagues was rarely strong. If individual performance review in a formal sense, or development discussions, were part of the organizational philosophy it seemed very rare indeed that these were carried out between the chief executive and subordinate directors. The common perception seemed to be that once people arrived at the main board such processes were unnecessary, dangerous and unproductive.

While some subordinate directors agreed with this view, a significant number did not. They thought that chief executives ought to carry out with them the processes which they in turn were required to carry out with their subordinates. They did not necessarily want the same processes exactly, but they did want an organized discussion with an appropriate amount of time. Several directors in different organizations used almost exactly the same words:

> The chief executive will tell you that I know what he thinks about me and that he has talked to me about my performance. A ten-minute discussion in the car on the way to the airport doesn't seem to me to be a proper performance review, and certainly there has never been any discussion of my development.

The chief executive might actually learn something relevant to his own needs from such discussions.

Nearly all the chief executives and chairmen we saw recognized their responsibility for encouraging improved management development. The fact that they do not try to establish the development needs of their immediate subordinates clearly is not helpful. Some chief executives would find a discussion a formidable prospect, and indeed we were told that a number had explicitly rejected opportunities presented by the personnel director. Some might however be prepared to put a toe in the water by picking out perhaps the most recently arrived member of the board for such a discussion, rather than leaping into discussions with all their colleagues, some of whom might be older if not wiser, and might also have been competitors for the job the chief executive now filled.

Managers concentrate on task performance rather than development because that is how they derive their intrinsic satisfactions, and because they are rewarded and recognized by peers and bosses on the basis of their managerial and professional expertise. The more explicit the chief executive can make the rewards to those directors and managers who do engage in the development of others, whether through Type 3 or Type 2 development, the more likely it is that those activities will thrive and produce useful results for the organization.

The chief executive also has a responsibility for the system rather than just relationships with individual subordinates. Many indeed recognized the former but not the latter. They ought therefore to ensure that the management development policy and system are discussed, and could now do so using the insights available in this book. They ought to ensure that management development for the top is discussed on the main board at least once a year. It should also be included directly in other important management meetings, for example on the business plan or budget.

Many boards use a committee of non-executive directors to review the remuneration of main board directors. We encountered no similar committee dealing with the development of the top resource in the business! The decision of the main board of a company in which I worked to review top level succession and development once a year had a stimulating effect on the seriousness with which the whole process was regarded. Such a review would provide alternative ways of deciding the successor to the chief executive himself, and perhaps ensure that such a successor was developed as well as identified.

Interestingly, the study by Stieglitz refers to the fact that identifying a successor is regarded as the prime task by chief executives; they do not seem to have talked about developing one. Some of the problems of identifying and developing a successor are illustrated by the success and failure of an American and a Japanese company in the book by Pascale and Athos.[3] What criteria are to be used? In particular, is the organization looking for a mirror image or avoiding one? Does it seek to develop one successor or several? The different experiences of Geneen at ITT and Matsushita should make fascinating and perhaps disturbing reading for any chief executive.

Actions by directors on their own behalf

As with chief executives, it is important that directors keep themselves up to date, refreshing their ideas and improving their appreciation of issues. They too have to test the past learning which has taken them into their current jobs against the challenges of new situations which they may not have encountered on the way. They need to learn new processes for handling relatively familiar problems, and processes for dealing with new problems. At the most basic level, for example, directors in the 1980s need to know about Information Technology in the same way that their predecessors of 20 years ago needed to learn about computers.

While much of this book is intended to show how managers and directors can learn from the present, they also have to learn to manage the future. Many of the directors we saw did not perceive the further development of their abilities as a significant current priority. Our discussions showed that both the need and the opportunity for such development were greater than some directors realized.

Checking needs

Directors should therefore check any areas of their work in which they can improve their personal performance. They might choose to challenge the conventional wisdom that their performance and development needs are not reviewed by the chief executive or chairman. While not being prepared to initiate such discussion, some chief executives would certainly respond. Directors might also seek feedback from colleagues or even perhaps subordinates. It would of course be necessary to choose someone able to convey difficult information sensitively. A third possibility is to go outside the immediate management stream. This might be done through a colleague in another business, an ex-boss working somewhere else, or perhaps by using one of the specialists in management development available in consultancies or management educational institutions.

This is the organized approach to personal development. However, we know that many directors will not see their priorities for personal action in this form. It may therefore be more helpful to turn to the activities in which they could be involved as directors to see how they might be exploited for development benefit.

Informal problem-solving

Undoubtedly people learn from one another a great deal of the time by informal exchanges about the tasks they are performing and the problems they are facing. Such exchanges are rarely seen as specifically asking for advice and therefore would often not be seen as 'learning', although a form of learning may often occur. We encountered a particular kind of exchange which seemed to us particularly relevant for directors who might be reluctant to ask for advice directly. Perhaps they would call in on a colleague to discuss a problem without overtly asking for guidance, but nonetheless receive comments about past events, alternative solutions or a projected solution offered by the director.

Even more interesting was the arrangement in some organizations whereby directors met regularly but informally, for example at 9.00 am every Monday. These meetings had none of the bureaucracy of formal management processes – no secretary, no minutes and no clear decisions. They were designed to facilitate an exchange of views. While explicitly designed to help directors carry out formal tasks they were recognized in our discussions as sometimes having a significant informal learning element. They involved the same exchange of experiences, pursuit of facts and testing of ideas in debate which can be found on good quality management programmes. The cases quoted to us seemed to combine the best aspects of challenge with the necessary features of support for learning to occur. Locating the directors' offices all on one floor often aided the most informal process, in which individuals shared problems.

Using an outside mentor

A few directors made significant use of a personal contact outside the business who acted as counsellor and guide. They might discuss career plans from time to time, but more often they would discuss particular problems and opportunities. In many ways the process is similar to that mentioned in the previous paragraph, but use of an outsider removes the problems of competition and perceptions about individual performance which make some in-company discussions rather difficult. Some directors used contacts from a course in this informal way.

External activities

Most work outside the organization seems to be taken on because it is useful to have a presence, for example, on an industrial committee in order to collect information or seek influence; individuals also participate outside for personal satisfaction and recognition.

Development benefits can also be obtained. One director had himself nominated for an external committee largely concerned with marketing in his industry, because his own background was largely financial and this was a way of extending his knowledge. Other directors identified particular benefits derived from encountering major representatives of their industry, powerful civil servants and occasionally ministers. Such experiences can sensibly be used as opportunities to learn, and will be more effective if identified in advance.

Sir John Harvey-Jones, then Chairman of ICI, made an interesting comment in the *Financial Times* of February 5th 1986:

> We are an inbred company. Most of us have spent our lives in ICI. Non-executive posts give us the experience of a totally different type though hopefully we pay our way. One might be in a company that is party to a takeover, or has cash flow problems. These are experiences we would rather learn at someone else's expense.

Reading and discussing

Reading, as we have seen, is not high on the list of ways in which most directors learn. They found it difficult enough to keep up with internal paperwork and with what they saw as high priority material about their industry or customers. We believe that a number of directors actually missed opportunities to learn even from the reading they do. We encountered for example directors who read articles from management journals such as *Management Today* and *Harvard Business Review* with some regularity. At the time of our survey the two most frequently read management books were *In Search of Excellence* and *Iacocca*. Sometimes they passed on articles or books to colleagues or subordinates.

Such directors could get more value out of their reading by discussing it. This should extend beyond a casual comment or two over lunch. An individual director could propose such a discussion to a like-minded colleague or to the board as a group. Ideas in the book and the reaction of colleagues to them would both be debated and the relevant lessons more effectively learned.

Attending courses

Many directors do not consider attending either internal or external courses. One reason is that of status, and the second usually an unwillingness to spend time in this way on an experience often perceived to have little immediate application.

The problem of status is met, if at all, by attending an external instead of an internal course. Very few directors had attended anything important after reaching main board level. A few had attended short-duration programmes. The benefits claimed were normally the sharing of problems with colleagues at the same level, developing useful contacts and having a chance to think through some of their problems in depth. Even short programmes of this kind can assist in providing the individual director with a change in perspective, a different set of solutions and sometimes the opportunity to stand back and reflect on what is going on in his organization. Particularly for those directors who have been many years in a single organization, there is the additional benefit of getting outside their familiar environment.

We found a few directors who had been stimulated by sharing an internal course with their colleagues on the board. Sometimes this was an abbreviated version of a course being offered lower down in the organization, sometimes one designed specifically for the board

members. For some this was a way of catching up with learning they
had missed in earlier years.

Reviewing the team

Occasionally a complete team of executive directors had reviewed
their collective performance, relationships and working processes.
Such reviews had immediate application and also involved useful
learning about problems and methods of overcoming them.

In Chapter 3 the actual and potential contribution of colleagues
and subordinates was mentioned. Nearly all of the learning process
had been Type 1, that is wholly informal, accidental and relatively
unaware. There is a lesson here also for directors who move into the
Type 2 mode in which they become more consciously aware of the
wide variety of opportunities. As one director said: 'I have very
good people working for me. Some of them know much more than I
do about some subjects or problems. I ask them questions and listen
hard.'

What should directors do for subordinates?

Chief executives rarely reviewed the performance of their directors
formally and considered development openly with them. Directors
themselves were more likely to engage in this process with subordinates. This is Type 3 Management Development, part of the formal process of considering needs, identifying opportunities and
taking action. The reluctance of directors to appraise is fairly
widespread. Appraisal however presents major opportunities as
well as particular difficulties. As indicated in Chapter 7, much has
been written about this process and advice is available on why to do
it and how to do it well. Rather than spend time flicking the whip on
this particular horse, therefore, it is better for the purposes of this
book to deal with the more unusual issues involved in developing
managers through Type 2 processes.

Identifying learning opportunities.

The directors' responsibility for encouraging Type 2 processes lies in offering a model showing the directors' own willingness to learn from such processes, and giving counsel, advice and direction to subordinate managers on how they too can benefit from then. This does not imply trying to convert every task process into a learning process as well; although this could be theoretically justified, it is quite outside the realms of realistic managerial priorities.

The encouragement of learning by directors means trying to identify the most significant occasion on which learning can be derived from the task. It means occasionally placing learning overtly on the agenda by, for example, asking participants to review what they have learned from discussion of particular problems at meetings. They might do it by suggesting an open discussion at the end of a meeting, or simply that all those present make some notes about the most important issues. We found a few directors for whom such a reviewing process had been a powerful part of their learning history. Although it suits some managers, and some learning styles, more than others it is a process which many managers could adopt.

Using meetings and projects

Problem-solving meetings and working on projects were constantly brought home to us as crucial to the learning experiences identified. Sometimes projects can be designed and used explicitly as development experiences – but that makes them Type 3 experiences. The more frequently encountered phenomenon, as we showed earlier, is a Type 1 development experience in which managers participate in projects without being aware of the learning implications because they are simply seen as tasks. Directors can help to convert them into Type 2 phenomena by spelling out some of the potential development issues in advance of the project, discussing what is happening during the project with the manager involved, and reviewing afterwards what has been achieved. Factors which might be involved include working with someone from outside the company for the first time, working with a consultant, visiting different organizations and working in new countries.

It is impossible to over-emphasize the richness of the experience gained by our directors from the major projects they had been involved in, and the breadth of the learning from particular problem-solving meetings. Having recognized how inefficient the process of learning had been at the time, they commented frequently on how much more could have been gained if only someone had taken the trouble to identify the opportunities for them. Some of them added that they should have seen the opportunities for themselves!

Learning from a boss

Of all the comments made to us about learning from the boss (a sadly infrequent occasion apparently) one fact came over most clearly. The boss who provides the best development opportunities is the boss who provides some space. As one director put it to us, 'he always allowed me to try and swim; but he would not have let me drown'. As another put it, 'He always wanted my ideas and my solutions first; that made me stretch and expand. An earlier boss was constantly telling me what his views were, which made it difficult for me to think differently.'

The directors who felt that they had been significantly helped by a boss sometimes identified early experiences: being shown how to write a good report, problem analysis, going through an in-tray. Later experiences changed in form and ceased to be tutorial. Sometimes a boss would leave a problem untackled for a time to see who would volunteer to pick it up. Sometimes he would assign a problem or project directly to a manager, who might not previously have been involved. Such assignments were often task-centred, sometimes with the implications of a test: 'if you can do this it will show us what you are made of'. A good development boss would convert these informal unstructured experiences into informal structured experiences by discussing the development possibilities in them.

These illustrations show the need for directors to see the opportunities for development within normal management processes, and to give more attention to them without burdening them with a formal requirement.

Mentoring

Although most of the directors had not had a 'mentor' experience, we found some important places where they were themselves acting in this capacity. We are not concerned here so much with the mentor as door opener, a feature which has a great many dangers as well as possible benefits. We found a few illustrations of a more direct personal relationship which we thought important. Organizations were encouraging directors to carry through a sort of half-way house on mentoring. They were not introducing formal mentoring schemes with all the process of training mentors. Nor were they relying entirely on individual directors picking up individual managers accidentally. Instead they were encouraging the mentoring process by asking each director to pick up several managers at different levels in the organization. They were expected to have informal discussions and to talk with them about their development. Whilst again there must be dangers in having some sort of 'Crown Prince' identification, there is a significant advantage in this kind of mentoring. It avoids the dangers of formalizing the process to the extent that it becomes an unwanted obligation, leading perhaps to the problems of a formal management development scheme. Equally it gives encouragement to directors to carry out in a personal way some of their normal responsibilities: 'I have a group of 14 in whom I take a particular interest. I see them regularly, offer advice and guide their progress.'

Some of the learning processes which have been suggested for directors could also be undertaken by managers. Processes which can be developed by managers for themselves include:

Learning from problem-solving

One of the most important ways in which managers learn is through the experience of dealing with managerial problems. The most effective managers seem to learn from these experiences by:

> assessing carefully the nature of the problem
> testing this assessment with colleagues or boss
> identifying and testing solutions
> reviewing the extent to which the preferred solution worked
> analysing why the solution did or did not work

However, this rational approach is too extensive for most managers most of the time. Nor do they see most problems as being worth the kind of analytical effort we have just described. A sensible learning step for managers is to set themselves an objective of learning from problems:

1   They might want to select a particular kind of problem, perhaps something new to them.

2   They might choose to concentrate on one stage of these problem-solving processes to see what they can learn.

They may decide that the learning objective is connected with the ability to put over an analysis of the problem to their boss. Or alternatively they may decide that they are likely to learn most from implementation.

Though managers are more inclined to learn by analysis of failure it is actually desirable to learn by analysing the causes of success, not least because what has succeeded in one situation may not succeed in another. If however you are more motivated to do the former, stay with it.

Learning from projects

Most managers are sometimes placed on projects outside their normal range of work activities. These appointments are normally made because the manager is best suited from a task point of view, rather than as a specific development experience. We found many examples including:

> reviewing international opportunities with other firms in the industry
> problems of entering the Japanese market
> defining a new management information system
> visiting acquired companies and recommending action
> establishing a factory on a green field site
> working with external consultants

The manager who recognizes development possibilities even within an apparently task-centred appointment can speed up and improve his learning processes by:

> picking out the least familiar aspects of the project and deciding how to improve his knowledge of them

experimenting with different kings of personal or managerial action, and seeing what the results are

reviewing the activities of colleagues on the project and seeing which of them are being successful in their task within the project and why.

analysing the leadership processes of the person running the project and deciding which are effective and which ineffective

Learning by reviewing the job

If managers are already working to a defined list of clearly stated objectives, with standards of achievement or priorities for the year, they have a natural basis for assessing success or failure. Many managers, however, lack this immediate guidance. They may set their own objectives and priorities which they feel unable to communicate with their boss (an undesirable but occasionally necessary situation). Analysis of the reason for success or failure within those priorities, or success or failure on particularly important tasks, is the learning process involved.

Whereas this first suggestion involves taking a fairly broad view of the year, it is also possible to review your achievements on a weekly or even a daily basis.

Sharing management action

We found very few directors with experience of being formally coached in dealing with a management issue. We found many more with experience of working through a problem with a boss or occasionally a colleague. The process includes:

seeing how someone else would handle a particular issue

testing your ideas against theirs

using them as a sounding board for proposals you may want to make elsewhere.

All these processes are part of the normal management activity. They are also capable, if you wish them to be, of being used as learning influences. What have you learned from the experience of sharing a problem with a colleague? What caused your boss to respond to you in the way he did? What kind of things will you do next time?

Setting up your own process

Managers are more likely than chief executives and directors (particularly nowadays) to be involved in the formal processes described as Type 3. Each manager should look at the management development processes discussed in Chapters 6 and 7, all of which should be available, at least potentially, through any organization. Each manager should consider which of them are currently available and decide why some of them are not. What can you do about the ones not apparently available to you? Here are some possible actions:

1   If your boss has never given you a counselling session in which he discussed your performance and your career possibilities, is that something you have to accept, or something you could ask him to rectify?

2   Is there a respected person in the business who might be interested in having informal discussions with you, in acting as your mentor?

3   Do you have to be entirely responsive to other people's ideas on your next job, or can you indicate what you would like to do?

4   Can you produce an individual development plan for yourself? Does it have to be done on your own, or is it something you can share with a colleague? Is there a professional resource you can call in to help you do it?

Experience with courses

Chapters 5 and 6 discussed the influence of courses. Not all are

effective for all individuals, and some are not effective at all. Sometimes courses are offered as a panacea, as a solution to a problem
which cannot be resolved by a course. In spite of these qualifica-
tions, well-designed courses can be powerful and uniquely appropriate aids. Once the need for a particular skill is established courses
can dramatically improve performance. Given the significance
attached by most directors to the selection of managers, work on the
skills involved is most easily tackled on a course. Areas of business
outside the experience of the individual or indeed of the organization can often be tackled best by courses. Our experience on this
survey supports the view that directors have been reaching the top
under-trained, and may still be doing so. There is a need for effective training combined with other effective development processes.

Since we found so many 'grey' comments about the usefulness of
courses, it is sensible to look at the reasons. Managers are still sent
on courses without commitment or understanding of the reasons
for them. Some organizations operate a catalogue, and managers
are taken through it. While this is beneficial in terms of ensuring
that all individuals in an organization have some basic training, it is
not in keeping with modern ideas of allowing managers to direct
their own development.

Managers hooked on the catalogue might like to experiment. A
simple rejection of a course might have disadvantageous consequences for them within the organization. They might rather consider asking for an alternative learning process which better suited
their needs in terms of content, or alternatively which suited their
learning style better. Instead of simply declining to go on a course,
perhaps they could volunteer to learn about marketing by being
attached to the marketing department for ten half-days.

Managers in an organization where there is total disbelief in the
virtues of courses may have an even more difficult task. Since the
argument is often about time and money, they may be able to loosen
up the decision-making process by finding some equivalent in an
apparently costly management operation and asking that the same
sort of money be spent on a course.

Choosing a management development adviser

Organizations which take Type 3 Management Development

seriously will want to have some professional advice on how to undertake it, usually provided either through a personnel director or a management development adviser. An adviser needs to know about and be able to implement Type 3 development. Often ignored, not least because management development advisers themselves have not been aware of the opportunities, is the capacity to handle Type 2 development.

One specification is important for both: whoever is chosen ought to have developed someone personally as his or her managerial responsibility. This may seen a difficult specification but it is a necessary part of both experience and credibility. Secondly, if the adviser is to be acceptable outside the demonstrated formal areas of Type 3 development it is worth enquiring whether they have ever had the crucial managerial responsibility for actually sacking someone.

It may seen strange to give so much emphasis to the ability of advisers to deal with Type 2 Management Development since their role might be seen primarily in Type 3. The point of course is that part of their roles as management development adviser will be to encourage managers into the Type 2 process without taking the design and implementation responsibility needed for Type 3 processes.

References

1   Bennis, W. and Nanus, B., *Leaders*, Harper & Row, New York, 1985
2   Stieglitz, H., *Chief Executives View Their Jobs*, Conference Board, New York, 1985
3   Pascale, R. and Athos, A., *The Art of Japanese Management*, Penguin Books, London, 1982

14 Advice to advisers

There are broadly three groups of advisers who might be able to help organizations develop people for the top jobs:

personnel directors and management development advisers

external consultants

management education and training centres

Personnel directors and management development advisers

A number of organizations had no clear policy or practices for developing people for the main board, or indeed for any management positions. Many remain to be convinced about the value of any formalized approach. Some of them have never considered the matter seriously, presumably because they feel themselves to have suffered no damage. All too often a failure to plan, particularly for the top jobs, leads either to disastrous appointments from inside or to expensive and risky recruitment from outside. Organizations which currently do no Type 3 Management Development ought therefore to consider how they expect directors to develop and whether there is a case for at least some elements of Type 3 processes.

Most other areas of the business are nowadays subject to planning. Even if formal training and development are not seen as appropriate for the mass of employees, the view that the development of the people in the most important jobs in the organization can be left to chance ought to be formally reconsidered. A decision should be based on the facts rather than on no analysis at all.

A more formal, more planned approach in the Type 3 mode does not necessarily mean a huge volume of forms, meetings, sending people off on courses and all the other worries often expressed, particularly by smaller organizations. Planning on a limited scale, perhaps through a once-a-year review of key managers, might be a legitimate answer for some organizations.

Sometimes there are Type 3 Management Development processes at subsidiary levels in the organization, but no process exists for integrating decisions about people for the main board. Such organizations ought to consider the points made in Chapter 7 as to whether complete delegation of these decisions serves their longer term interests.

Organizations already operating a formalized Type 3 approach should review the objectives, processes and results of the management development schemes as they apply to the top level. They need to ask the following questions:

> Is management development for the top jobs on the agenda for discussion at main board at least once a year? Are there other top level meetings at which it should be discussed, eg Business Plan meetings?

> Presuming our management development scheme is intended to produce enough directors of the right quality at the right time, has it in the past achieved that objective?

> How far have the processes and the principles of our scheme applied in reality to our current directors, and how influential have they been in their development?

> Does our management development system actually provide a range of opportunities and alternatives, or is it limited essentially to one type of process (eg job rotation or courses).

> Is there a statement of what we expect directors to do well, and a consequential statement of development processes appropriate to those needs?

How far are decisions about job moves influenced by considerations of individual development? Are such moves discussed and identified not only with personnel and the relevant top manager but also with the person who is to be developed?

Do the management development processes we use differ according to the different development needs of individuals and their different preferences for learning processes?

How far do the courses we presently use for our managers deal with the reality of management rather than abstract concepts about it?

Do these courses help managers to learn more effectively after the course?

What definition do we currently have of management development, and would we now change it to embrace the three types of management development on which this book is based?

What are we doing for our existing directors?

How might the principles and details set out in this book be discussed with directors, manager and personnel advisers?

The detailed review of formal management development processes given in Chapters 6 and 7 should be a major help in considering these questions. The charts headed 'Levers for success' (Figure 7.2) and 'Causes of failure' (Figure 7.3) provide a direct means of checking both the history and current situation of Type 3 development.

This book has largely advocated working with the grain of managerial reality instead of against it. This may be a difficult proposition for some personnel people, whose actions probably reflect the same combination of influences that affects directors, including their own development, their skills, the things the organization values and their own personal values. Personnel directors' beliefs about the development of managers, as demonstrated by their statements and actions, would be something like the following:

Managers are not born, they are not made, but they can be developed.

Most managers do not carry out properly their responsibility
for the development of other managers; if left to themselves
not much of value would happen.

It is therefore necessary to set up systems for management
development through which the processes of developing
managers are organized and planned.

The effectiveness of such systems depends to a very large
degree on the commitment of top management; that commitment is often difficult to obtain.

Directors themselves ought to be the jewel in the crown in
terms of management development processes, illustrating the
benefits of formal management development by their demonstrated personal capacity.

Personnel advisers should not give up their beliefs about the virtues
of Type 3 Management Development. It is not necessary to abandon
Type 3 in order to take up Type 2; the two can and should be complementary. What is required is a broader view of what can be
attempted in management development, and the perception that
there are more opportunities for improving the development of
managers through Type 2 than can be provided by sole reliance on
Type 3.

The argument is essentially about integration. The system of
management development ought to be an integrated approach in
the sense of ensuring that learning is directed to and through
managerial reality, and that Type 3 and Type 2 Management
Development are brought together. The process of integration may
be from Type 3 into Type 2 as opportunities of a Type 2 variety are
identified and worked on in Type 3 experiences. It may equally be
from Type 2 to Type 3 as the identification of more learning and
development opportunities in the job persuades managers that
some of them would be better dealt with by off-the-job Type 3
processes.

From the personnel adviser's perspective, the clearest opportunity is obviously to use Type 3 processes to generate enthusiasm
and capacity for Type 2 development processes. As I have already
shown, courses (for example) can be designed as gateways to
Type 2 experiences.

Personnel advisers must find appropriate ways of raising questions about the development of current directors. The unwilling-ness of many chief executives to review the performance of directors, still less to look at their development needs, is understan-dable but in many organizations ought to be challenged. The per-sonnel adviser might make the comments given in the previous chapter (page 216) directly to the chief executive, and to directors, as a means of raising discussion about the process. Much the best approach would be to persuade directors themselves that they actually want the issue to be raised. If the personnel adviser approaches the chief executive without such support, it is likely that he will give many of the familiar reasons why discussion is neither appropriate nor wanted.

We encountered two personnel directors who had been asked by their chief executive to act on his behalf in discussing performance and development issues with their colleagues. Neither organiza-tions nor individual directors can afford to assume that those at the top have become so fully developed or so atrophied that no further learning is possible.

An alternative is to go outside the organization to undertake this kind of discussion. It may be the only way of achieving it, so if the purpose is seen as important enough the cost will be a secondary issue. For people at the top, making the most significant decisions in the business, an investment in improving their capacity to perform can pay off dramatically. As the personnel director involved in one of the cases put it to us, the cost of individual counselling of this kind is trivial in comparison with the money the director concerned is spending every day, and the profits he can generate through better decisions.

In these instances personnel advisers are acting as the experts on potential external resources. Many of them are used to the idea of helping an organization to choose courses. Under the suggested new framework their responsibilities would be extended. Firstly, they would need to assess the extent to which any courses met the needs of the business not only in content relevance and managerial reality but in aiding the Type 2 process. Secondly, they would need to review the abilities and track record of external advisers. Person-nel advisers must represent these new ideas about management development effectively not only as advisers but as personal prac-titioners. They must first have a full understanding of the learning and development processes as they apply to individuals. Generalized solutions to generalized problems encounter the reality of that supremely interesting phenomenon, the individual human being. It is the job of the advisers to help individuals to select and experience those processes from which they will learn effectively, and then help them to learn whatever process is chosen.

Advisers must represent on their own account, through personal action and through actions undertaken with any subordinate staff, the processes of Type 3 development which they wish other managers to take up. Advisers unable to demonstrate such personal commitment and effectiveness will receive what is delightfully known in America as a Bronx Cheer.

Finally, and perhaps most difficult of all, advisers must get to know a great deal about the managerial game as distinct from organizing their own Type 3 Management Development game. Unless the advisers are aware in general terms of the kind of managerial activities open to Type 2 development (it will be impossible for them to know the detail of every particular event), advice about Type 2 will not be very influential. Such knowledge might be acquired through formal Type 3 activities, such as reading and attending courses. It might be gained perhaps even more effectively through Type 2 processes, particularly by seeking opportunities to be involved in and learn from managerial activities. This may mean pursuing invitations to attend meetings or participate in task groups where there is no very strong requirement for personnel presence. Although there might be some conflict over priorities, and certainly advisers will not want to convey the view that they have nothing better to do, there is nothing more flattering than to say to a manager that you actually want to learn more about management processes.

External consultants

Many of the requirements for external consultants to operate effectively are the same as those for personnel advisers. Extension from Type 3 activities into Type 2 will perhaps be more difficult for them because they are more likely to be occasional visitors to an organization rather than permanently present. The opportunity therefore for noticing and suggesting action on Type 2 opportunities may be more limited. It is perhaps tempting for external advisers to operate as purely Table 3 influencers. They may feel more secure both personally and economically in offering the kind of packages often associated with Type 3 development.

However, those external consultants who are concerned to help with effective management development rather than with doing their own familiar thing will want to seek ways in which Type 3 activities can be used to generate Type 2 opportunities. They will have to build into their Type 3 processes examples of and discussions about Type 2 processes. For an external consultant who would like the satisfaction of real results, and perhaps a more extended relationship with managers than Type 3 processes often provide, Type 2 Management Development offers a challenging opportunity.

Management education and training centres

The main message for management education and training centres has already been provided in Chapters 5 and 6. If such centres concentrate on management reality and use it they will have started the process of making themselves effective. If they add to that a concern to help managers to learn by looking at the learning process, they will have added the second dimension. If, having improved their own Type 3 offerings through such a major shift of attention, they then use their Type 3 activities to show managers how to use Type 2, management education centres will be influencing managerial effectiveness through improved managerial learning processes.

While I believe these proposals are logical and essential I do not regard them as easy for the staff of such centres. Many of them seem more interested in displaying their own knowledge than in attempting to meet the real concerns of managers with whom they are working. Nor is this knowledge wholly irrelevant or unwanted; it is the proportion of attention that needs to be changed.

It is however a significant shift in philosophy. Those institutions which are the custodians of structured learning experiences must do far more to ensure that the learning experience is more satisfactory for more managers exposed to them. That ought not to be as dramatically difficult a step as the lack of interest in the learning process in most educational institutions suggests. Many educationalists and trainers want to play their own game with managers on their own terms. Perhaps I am optimistic in assuming that the best and brightest would prefer to play the managers' game, because that is the game that really needs to be won.

If nothing else, read ...

Although a large number of references are attached to the separate chapters of this book, a relatively small number of books are absolutely essential. Some of the central themes of this book are revealed in the following:

> *The General Managers* by John Kotter (Free Press 1982)
> *Choices for the Manager* by Rosemary Stewart (McGraw-Hill 1982)
> *Making Experience Pay* by Alan Mumford (McGraw-Hill 1980)
> *Learning to Learn For Managers* by Alan Mumford (MCB University Press 1986)

Read them!

Index

242 INDEX

Political influences 169-70
Potential review 100
Problem-solving 47-9, 219, 223,
    225-6
Product influence 30
Professional qualification 14
Profit centre 31-2, 97
Programme management
    organizational system 196
Programmed knowledge 180
Projects 20-1, 223, 226-7
Promotion 107-9
Psychological reward 6
Pushing at the boundaries 20

Questioning 180

Reading 50-1, 220-1
Refinement stage 34
Replacement plans 95
Research 124, 130-7
Reshaping stage 34
Resource plans 95
Reviewing achievements 19
Rewards 7, 165, 188
Risk taking 168
Role cultures 103-4
Role plays 195

Sales volume 2
Schooling 5
Secondment 28-9
Self-analysis 64
Self-assessment 202
Self-development 64, 112, 202
Self-initiated experience 112
Size effects 164
Special assignments 22-3
Strategic skills 140
Subordinates, learning from 62
Succession plans 95, 96
Survey, participants in 1-2

Taking hold stage 34
Task forces 21
Teams 138
Technology as managerial
    influence 164
Travel 139-40
Trust 64-5

University education 5
Unlearning 180

Women 174
    directors 12-13